PuNK

pretty

in PuNk

etty

# pretty in punk

25 PUNK, ROCK, and GOTH knitting projects

By ALYCE BENEVIDES and JAQUELINE MILLES
Photographs by ROB BENEVIDES

CHRONICLE BOOKS
SAN FRANCISCO

Library of Congress
Cataloging-in-Publication
Data:

Benevides, Alyce.
Pretty in punk : 25 punk, rock,
    and goth knitting projects /
    by Alyce Benevides and
    Jaqueline Milles; photographs
    by Rob Benevides.
p. cm.

isbn-13: 978-0-8118-5744-4
isbn-10: 0-8118-5744-1

1. Knitting—Patterns.
2. Punk culture.
I. Milles, Jaqueline. II. Title.

TT820.B48 2007
746.43'2041—dc22
2006029654

MANUFACTURED IN
China

DESIGNED BY
Lesley Feldman

CRAFT DESIGNS
Alyce Benevides and
Jaqueline Milles of
KNIT-HEAD
www.knit-head.com

PHOTOGRAPHY &
ART DIRECTION
Rob Benevides,
Benefex Studio

PHOTO ASSISTANT
AND WARDROBE
Alyce Benevides

ILLUSTRATIONS
Alyce Benevides
and Jaqueline Milles

HAIR & MAKEUP
Eun Oh

ADDITIONAL HAIR
& MAKEUP
Jaqueline Milles
and Michael Laudati

Distributed in Canada
by Raincoast Books
9050 Shaughnessy Street
Vancouver, British Columbia
V6P 6E5

10 9 8 7 6 5 4 3 2 1

Chronicle Books LLC
680 Second Street
San Francisco, California
94107

www.chroniclebooks.com

dedicated to my loving and talented husband, rob benevides, for believing
in me and inspiring me from the moment we met. to my late "grammy" alice m. buttermark,
a writer in her own right and the person who sparked my alice in wonderland obsession.
to my family, especially my late father-in-law, robert benevides sr.,
who always supported our artistic endeavors. finally, to my late friend mary tighe,
an artist who embodied the true spirit of punk rock.

— Alyce Benevides

dedicated to my family —
shahla, jan, caroline, matthew, eric, tristan, and liam;
to the memory of mamanjan and aghajan;
and to the memory of opa — i'd like to think he
passed down his crafty gene to me.

— jaqueline milles

# COnTEnTs

## FOR THE
### CHaPTer 01
# head

## FOR THE
### CHaPTer 02
# neck

## foR The
### CHaPTer 03
# chest

# FOR THE CHAPTER 04
## arms

# FOR THE CHAPTER 05
## bum

# FOR THE CHAPTER 06
## rest

### REsoURcEs

pretty *in* PuNk

## WE CAME OF AGE IN THE 1980S. THAT SHOULD EXPLAIN A LOT RIGHT THERE.

*as teens in suburban new jersey, we were hit by the raw energy and subversive style of punk. we idolized everything from the u.k. we watched* the young ones, *listened to punk and new wave, and even adopted the occasional british accent. we read* bogey's *and* smash hits, *receiving them by mail weeks after their publication. our hair colors changed monthly. our parents groaned accordingly. we spent all of our money on concerts, and in the true spirit of punk rock, we ripped our clothes, took apart our seams, affixed safety pins, and painted our leather and denim jackets. we tore runs in our stockings, wore combat boots with skirts, and created looks all our own.*

*we stood out among our peers, and not always in a good way. some people thought we were a little strange, two of the few teenage girls in our high school who didn't have big perms or macy's credit cards. we didn't care. because we didn't want to look like everyone else, like those who shopped at the local malls and followed cookie-cutter dictates.*

*on weekends we hopped the train to new york city and soaked in the brilliant sights and sounds. overwhelmed, with blisters on our feet, we always went home exhausted yet inspired. punk-rock style has always appealed to us because of its edgy, do-it-yourself nature. we could take styles we admired and change them, making them our own.*

we began knitting together eleven years ago, long before needles and yarn became fashion accessories seen on movie sets and soho streets. sure, we began with the standard scarves and hats. we were novices. but soon we realized that our knitting skills didn't have to limit our expression or creativity. we took an unorthodox approach and experimented with outrageous colors, materials, and yarn textures. our creations were often bold in design, unlike most things in the mainstream knitting world. they were sexy, different, and fun, and when we wore our works, we were inevitably asked where we'd bought them. there are few things as satisfying as saying, "i made it myself."

that's why we started our knitting venture, knit-head, and that's how we came to write this book. in pretty in punk, we offer twenty-five original knit-head designs that even the most novice knitter can whip up—from hats that give you an instant mohawk hairdo to accessories that highlight your quirky side, from gothic-inspired styles to anglo-themed designs! you can make miniskirts, corsets, neckties, and more. we encourage you to follow our lead, duplicate us where you want, but remember to inject your own personality into everything you do. punk, in any art form, is about individuality.

SO HAVE A GO AT IT. RELEASE YOUR INNER ROCK STAR. ALL YOU NEED IS TWO STICKS AND A BALL OF YARN. ❤

CHaPTer 01

FoR THE head

*this is the signature hat of our company, knit-head. it was inspired in part by one of our favorite designers, the irreverent john galliano, as well as by the quintessential punk-rock hairstyle, the mohawk. after we presented depeche mode with these hats, the band added them to their onstage ensemble. this hat, most of all, captures our love of punk attitude and style.*

# punk's not dead

### felted earflap hat with i-cords and mohawk fringe

## MATERIALS

» Size 10 1/2 needles for small hat (size 11 for medium hat, size 13 for large hat), or size required to get correct gauge
» 2 stitch ring markers
» Row counter, optional
» Size 11 double-pointed needles
» Size 1 crochet hook
» Darning needle
» 2 skeins black bulky-weight wool yarn (Brown Sheep Co., Lamb's Pride Bulky, 85% wool, 15% mohair, Onyx, M05)
» 1 skein hot pink bulky-weight wool yarn (Brown Sheep Co., Lamb's Pride Bulky, 85% wool, 15% mohair, Lotus Pink, M38)

## GAUGE (IN STOCKINETTE STITCH)

» 13 stitches and 17 rows make a 4-inch square on size 10 1/2 needles, before felting
» 12 stitches and 16 rows make a 4-inch square on size 11 needles, before felting
» 11 stitches and 15 rows make a 4-inch square on size 13 needles, before felting

## FINISHED MEASUREMENTS

» Size small fits 18- to 20-inch head circumference
» Size medium fits 20- to 22-inch head circumference
» Size large fits 22-inch and larger head circumference

## SKILLS & METHODS

» Crochet (single)
» Felting
» Fringe
» I-cord
» Stockinette stitch

*continued »*

This hat is assembled out of 4 pieces. First, you will knit the 2 side pieces. Next, you will pick up stitches at the bottom edge of each piece and knit the earflaps directly on, finishing with an I-cord on both. Then you will attach the 2 sides by sewing them together along the center seam. Finally, you will attach a fringe to the end of each I-cord and 2 rows of staggered fringe on either side of the hat's center seam for the Mohawk.

To begin, cast on 30 stitches in black yarn on regular needles. Work in stockinette stitch for 21 rows. On the 22nd row (wrong side), place a stitch ring marker after the 14th stitch and after the 16th stitch. To create the rounded dome of the hat, there are 2 steps you will do simultaneously—decreases in the center as well as decreases on the side edges as follows:

*row 23:* Knit 2 together before first stitch marker and after second stitch marker; 28 stitches remain.

*row 24:* Purl without any decreasing; 28 stitches remain.

*row 25:* Knit 2 together at beginning and end of the row as well as before the first stitch marker and after the second stitch marker; 24 stitches remain.

*row 26:* Purl without any decreasing; 24 stitches remain.

*row 27:* Knit 2 together before the first stitch marker and after the second stitch marker; 22 stitches remain.

*row 28:* Purl 2 together at the beginning and end of the row; 20 stitches remain.

*row 29:* Knit 2 together before the first stitch marker and after the second stitch marker; 18 stitches remain.

*row 30:* Purl 2 together at the beginning and end of the row; 16 stitches remain.

*row 31:* Knit 2 together before the first stitch marker and after the second stitch marker; 14 stitches remain.

*row 32:* Purl 2 together at the beginning and end of the row; 12 stitches remain.

*row 33:* On this row, remove the stitch markers as you make your decreases. Knit 2 together twice at the beginning and end of the row; 8 stitches remain.

*row 34:* Purl 2 together at the beginning and end of the row; 6 stitches remain.

*row 35:* Bind off 6 stitches on this knit row.

To make the earflaps, use regular needles to pick up 17 stitches on the bottom edge of each piece, starting at the fourth stitch for the right side of the hat and the 9th stitch for the left side of the hat. Work 3 rows in stockinette stitch. For the side decreases, knit or purl 2 together at the beginning and end of rows 4, 7, 10, 12, 14, 15, and 16; 3 stitches remain. Transfer your knitting to size 11 double-pointed needles to make the I-cord. Take the needle with the knitting in your left hand, and slide all the stitches to the right end of the needle. Pull the yarn from the left side of the work across the back, and knit the first right-hand stitch. Knit to the end. Slide your work to the right end of the needle again, and repeat until the I-cord is approximately 12 inches long. Bind off.

Place the 2 pieces together, right sides facing each other, and stitch with a darning needle and about 20 inches of black yarn.

This seam joins the 2 halves of the hat. Weave all of the loose strands into the back of the knitting. Turn right-side out.

Now for the fun part! Fringe-mania!

You will cut individual strands of yarn to form fringes. Each strand should measure 8 inches. For the I-cords and Mohawk, you will need a total of 34 sets of fringe—1 set for each I-cord and 32 sets for the Mohawk. Each set consists of 4 pink strands and 6 black strands of yarn. To do this quickly and precisely, all you need is a 4-inch-by-4-inch piece of cardboard and a pair of scissors. Take the black yarn, hold its end at the bottom edge of the cardboard, and wrap the yarn around the cardboard 6 times. Snip it horizontally across the bottom. Next, take the pink yarn, and wrap it around the cardboard 4 times. Snip it horizontally across the bottom. Add these 4 strands of pink yarn to the 6 strands of black yarn, and you have your first set. Repeat 34 times.

For the I-cord, insert your crochet hook through 2 loops at the end of the I-cord. Fold 1 set of pink and black yarn in half. Hook the folded loop with your crochet hook, pull the loop through, and then pull all fringe ends through the loop to secure. Repeat this step to attach fringe to the end of the second I-cord.

And now for the pièce de résistance, the Mohawk. To begin your staggered fringes, begin on 1 side by inserting your crochet hook through the first stitch next to the seam in the fourth row. Hook, pull through toward you, and knot 1 set of fringe. The fringe knot should face the right side of the fabric. Following along the center seam, attach 1 fringe set every 4 rows. You will end up with

16 fringe sets on this side. Flip the hat over, and repeat as for the first side. Attach your second set of fringes on the opposite side of the center seam, in between the spaces created by the first set of 16 fringes. You will again end up with 16 fringe sets.

The last step is to felt the completed hat. We're not experts at felting, and we don't really do it for the felted effect. Rather, we discovered that taking a chance and throwing a knitted piece into the washing machine sometimes improves the overall texture and feel of the fabric. This is especially true when there is an intarsia design; the slight bit of felting smoothes out some of the edges of color changes. It also creates a sturdier-feeling fabric, which is great for bags and hats. For this hat in particular, it creates a fantastic texture in the Mohawk "hair." Please note that we encourage you to use your own favorite yarns to create these projects at home. However, you should be aware that synthetic fibers and superwash wools do not felt. If you'd like to create this look in acrylic yarn, we suggest using the wool/mohair blend yarn for the Mohawk and fringes only to achieve the same punk feel to the "hair."

To felt this project, throw it into a washing machine, and wash on a hot cycle with no detergent. Remove the hat from the washing machine, and get ready to get out some aggression. You will find each fringe set has gotten quite clumpy. Do not despair! Take your time separating each strand by grabbing the strands and tearing them apart, down to the knot. You are left with one charged Mohawk, and you didn't even have to shave your head! ❤

*don't let the bitter cold put a damper on your devilish demeanor.
this hat helps you stay warm while you're tempting fate!*

# lucky 13

felted earflap hat

## MATERIALS

» Size 10¹/₂ knitting needles (size 11
  for medium hat, size 13 for large hat),
  or size required to get correct gauge
» Yarn bobbins, optional
» 2 stitch ring markers
» Row counter, optional
» Darning needle
» Size H crochet hook
» 1 skein dark red bulky-weight wool yarn
  (Brown Sheep Co., Lamb's Pride Bulky,
  85% wool, 15% mohair, Spice, M145)
» 1 skein black bulky-weight wool yarn
  (Brown Sheep Co., Lamb's Pride Bulky,
  85% wool, 15% mohair, Onyx, M05)

## GAUGE (IN STOCKINETTE STITCH)

» 13 stitches and 17 rows make a
  4-inch square on size 10¹/₂ needles,
  before felting
» 12 stitches and 16 rows make
  a 4-inch square on size 11 needles,
  before felting
» 11 stitches and 15 rows make a
  4-inch square on size 13 needles,
  before felting

## FINISHED MEASUREMENTS

» Size small fits 18- to
  20-inch head circumference
» Size medium fits 20- to
  22-inch head circumference
» Size large fits 22-inch and
  larger head circumference

## SKILLS & METHODS

» Crochet (single)
» Duplicate stitch
» Felting
» Intarsia
» Stockinette stitch

*continued »*

**pretty** *in PuNk*

This hat is assembled out of 5 pieces. First, you knit the 2 red sides of the hat. The earflaps are then knit directly on, and everything is stitched onto the black racing stripe running down the center. Finally, a black border is crocheted on, and the number 13 is stitched onto the spades with a darning needle.

Before beginning your knitting, divide your yarn so that you have 2 equal-sized red balls of yarn. For the left side of the hat, begin by casting on 28 stitches in the red yarn on regular needles. Work intarsia in stockinette stitch for 23 rows as shown on the left-side spade intarsia graph. If you prefer, you can wind a few yards of the black yarn onto a yarn bobbin, but this intarsia is so simple, it's not too difficult to work with 3 balls of yarn. When the 23rd row is complete, cut the black yarn and 1 ball of red yarn. At this point you will need to begin a somewhat complicated set of decreases along the middle and ends of the work, so keep a piece of scrap paper handy. Place 2 stitch markers after the 13th stitch and after the 15th stitch on your needle in order to highlight the center seam along which your decreases will take place. You are essentially decreasing along a center seam every other row while simultaneously decreasing along the edges every third row 3 times, every other row 2 times, and then once again to end. One final note on the method of decreases: for the decreases along the ends of the work, we prefer to knit together the second and third stitch at the beginning of a row and the second- and third-to-last stitch at the end of a row in order to make a cleaner edge. Row-by-row instructions, rows 24 through 38:

*row 24:* Purl 2 together at the beginning and end of the row; 26 stitches remain.
*row 25:* Knit 2 together before the first stitch marker and after the second stitch marker; 24 stitches remain.
*row 26:* Purl without any decreasing; 24 stitches remain.

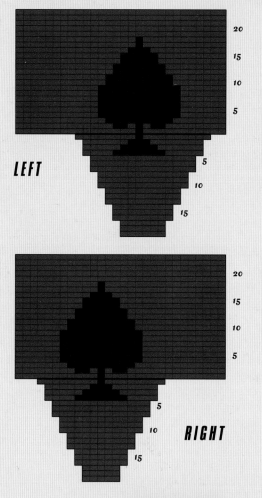

**LEFT**

**RIGHT**

**DARNING**

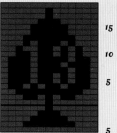

**row 27:** Knit 2 together at the beginning and end of the row as well as before the first stitch marker and after the second stitch marker; 20 stitches remain.

**row 28:** Purl without any decreasing; 20 stitches remain.

**row 29:** Knit 2 together before the first stitch marker and after the second stitch marker; 18 stitches remain.

**row 30:** Purl 2 together at the beginning and end of the row; 16 stitches remain.

**row 31:** Knit 2 together before the first stitch marker and after the second stitch marker; 14 stitches remain.

**row 32:** Purl without any decreasing; 14 stitches remain.

**row 33:** Knit 2 together at the beginning and end of the row as well as before the first stitch marker and after the second stitch marker; 10 stitches remain.

**row 34:** Purl without any decreasing; 10 stitches remain.

**row 35:** On this row, remove the stitch markers as you make your decreases. Knit 2 together at the beginning and end of the row as well as before the first stitch marker and after the second stitch marker; 6 stitches remain.

**row 36:** Purl without any decreasing; 6 stitches remain.

**row 37:** Knit 2 together at the beginning and end of the row; 4 stitches remain.

**row 38:** Bind off 4 stitches on this purl row.

For the right side, repeat as for the left, except follow the right-side intarsia graph. The picture is placed so that it is centered on the earflap and just off-center of the side of the hat.

For left earflap, take the left half of the hat, with the right side of the work facing you, and turn it upside down. Pick up 17 stitches along the edge of the hat with the red yarn, beginning at the fourth stitch. This counts as your first row of the earflap. Note that there is a slight break in the intarsia pattern of the bottom of the spade at this point. Do not worry—you will go back and correct this with a darning needle at the end. Beginning with the second row (wrong side), introduce the black yarn again and the second ball of red yarn, and follow the left intarsia graph while making decreases at the beginning and end of this row. Continue to work stockinette stitch, and decrease every third row until you have 5 stitches left. Bind off.

For the right earflap, follow the left-flap directions, with the exception of the location of the 17 picked-up stitches. For the right flap, begin picking up stitches at the ninth stitch from the left edge of the hat (see right intarsia graph).

To create the black racing stripe that acts as the center seam of your hat, cast on 4 stitches with the black yarn, and work in stockinette stitch for 76 rows. Bind off.

Using a darning needle and some black yarn, join all the pieces with black yarn using whatever sewing technique you prefer. Keep all pieces inside out as you assemble, so you have a neat finish when you turn the hat right-side out. After the joining, single crochet a row of black along the entire hat edge, earflaps included, with a crochet hook.

Your final detail is to embroider the number 13 on each side of the hat in red yarn using a darning needle and following the darning graph. The method we use is often referred to as a duplicate stitch. Simply insert the needle from the wrong side of the hat through the middle of the stitch located 1 below where the red duplicate stitch will end up. Pull yarn through, and insert from left to right along the 2 legs of the stitch 2 rows above the insertion point. Insert again back into the original point, and pull through. Repeat this as needed for coverage of each stitch where red should appear. Do this also with black yarn where the top of the spade stem should meet up with the bottom of the spade.

To felt, wash the hat by itself with no detergent in 1 cold water wash to shrink a bit and bring out the yarn's fuzzy texture. ♥

let the trickster in you take flight in our stylized version of the classic aviator cap. this hat was inspired by snoopy's red baron persona. as far as cartoon characters go, that dog has serious punk-rock attitude and style!

### red baron
*aviator cap*

### MATERIALS
» Size 10 1/2 knitting needles (size 11 for medium hat, size 13 for large hat), or size required to get correct gauge

» 2 stitch ring markers
» Row counter, optional
» Size 0 crochet hook
» Darning needle
» 1 snap fastener
» 1 skein off-white bulky-weight wool yarn (Brown Sheep Co., Lamb's Pride Bulky, 85% wool, 15% mohair, Oatmeal, M115)

» 1 skein red bulky-weight wool yarn (Brown Sheep Co., Lamb's Pride Bulky, 85% wool, 15% mohair, Blue Blood Red, M80)

### GAUGE (IN STOCKINETTE STITCH)
» 13 stitches and 17 rows make a 4-inch square on size 10 1/2 needles
» 12 stitches and 16 rows make a 4-inch square on size 11 needles
» 11 stitches and 15 rows make a 4-inch square on size 13 needles

### FINISHED MEASUREMENTS
» Size small fits 18- to 20-inch head circumference
» Size medium fits 20- to 22-inch head circumference
» Size large fits 22-inch and larger head circumference

### SKILLS & METHODS
» Crochet (single)
» Stockinette stitch

*continued »*

This hat is made up of 3 main pieces: 1 center and 2 sides. Earflaps are knit directly onto the bottom edge of each side piece. Each side piece is then joined to the center piece with a raised single crocheted seam. A single crochet trim is added around the edge of the hat, including the earflaps. Next, a 4-inch chinstrap is knit directly onto the bottom edge of the right earflap, and metal snap hardware is secured to the end of the chinstrap and the center bottom of the left earflap. Finally, 2 crocheted circles are attached over each earflap with a darning needle as an accent and for added warmth.

For the side pieces, cast on 24 stitches in off-white yarn. Work 22 rows in stockinette stitch. On the 22nd row (wrong side), place a stitch ring marker after the 14th stitch and after the 16th stitch. To create the rounded dome of the hat, there are 2 steps you will do simultaneously—decreases in the center as well as decreases on the side. Again, we suggest you knit 2 together on the second and third stitches for the beginning of the row or the second- and third-to-last stitches at the end of the row.

*row 23:* Knit 2 together before the first stitch marker and after the second stitch marker; 22 stitches remain.

*row 24:* Purl.

*row 25:* Knit 2 together at the beginning and end of the row, as well as before the first stitch marker and after the second stitch marker; 18 stitches remain.

*row 26:* Purl.

*row 27:* Knit 2 together before the first stitch marker and after the second stitch marker; 16 stitches remain.

*row 28:* Purl 2 together at the beginning and end of the row; 14 stitches remain.

*row 29:* Knit 2 together before the first stitch marker and after the second stitch marker; 12 stitches remain.

*row 30:* Purl 2 together at the beginning and end of the row; 10 stitches remain.

*row 31:* Knit 2 together before the first stitch marker and after the second stitch marker; 8 stitches remain.

*row 32:* Purl 2 together at the beginning and end of the row; 6 stitches remain.

*row 33:* Knit 2 together at the beginning and end of the row; 4 stitches remain.

Bind off. Repeat to create the second side piece.

For the center piece, cast on 8 stitches in the off-white yarn. Work 68 rows in stockinette stitch. Bind off.

For the earflaps, pick up the first 15 stitches for the right side and the last 15 stitches for the left side—these count as your first row of each earflap. Decrease by knitting 2 together at the beginning and end of every third row until you have 5 stitches left. Bind off.

To assemble, place the right side together with the center piece, wrong sides facing each other. With the red yarn, join the 2 pieces by single crocheting them together through every other stitch. This is an intentional raised seam. Repeat with the left side.

To tie the piece together, single crochet red trim into every other stitch around the perimeter of the hat.

For the chinstrap, pick up the 4 center stitches of the red trim at the base of the right earflap. Work 23 rows in stockinette stitch. Bind off.

To create the circle motifs, chain 2 with the red yarn. Single crochet 6 times into the first loop. Join the round with a slip stitch, and chain 1 to establish the next round. Single crochet twice into every stitch, making a 12-stitch round. Join the round with a slip stitch, and chain 1 to establish the next round. Work a single crochet stitch into the first stitch, then work 2 stitches into every other stitch to create an 18-stitch round. Join with a slip stitch, and chain 1 to establish the final round. Again, begin with a single crochet into the first stitch, then work 2 stitches into every other stitch to create a 27-stitch round. Join with a slip stitch, cut yarn leaving approximately 8 inches, and pull through to finish off. Repeat to create a second circle. Next, center each circle so that half is on the hat and half is on the earflap. Stitch the circles to the piece using your darning needle and the 8-inch strand of yarn. Turn the hat inside out, and weave all the loose ends into the back of the knitting.

To finish, we picked up an inexpensive snap kit at a local yarn shop and secured the top part of the snap to the end of the chinstrap and the base part to the bottom center of the left earflap. Feel free to do the same, or use a closure of your choice! ❤

red
baron

*a variation on our "punk's not dead" hat, this is the ultimate tribute to punk-rock music and the country that spawned many of our favorite bands, including the sex pistols. guaranteed to garner you stares, smiles, and more attention than you can handle!*

### MATERIALS

» Size 10$^1/_2$ needles for small hat (size 11 for medium hat, size 13 for large hat), or size required to get correct gauge
» Yarn bobbins, optional
» Row counter, optional
» Size 11 double-pointed needles
» Darning needle
» Size I crochet hook
» 1 skein blue bulky-weight wool yarn (Brown Sheep Co., Lamb's Pride Bulky, 85% wool, 15% mohair, Blue Boy, M79)
» 1 skein white bulky-weight wool yarn (Brown Sheep Co., Lamb's Pride Bulky, 85% wool, 15% mohair, Creme, M10)
» 1 skein red bulky-weight wool yarn (Brown Sheep Co., Lamb's Pride Bulky, 85% wool, 15% mohair, Ruby Red, M180)

### GAUGE (IN STOCKINETTE STITCH)

» 13 stitches and 17 rows make a 4-inch square on size 10$^1/_2$ needles, before felting
» 12 stitches and 16 rows make a 4-inch square on size 11 needles, before felting
» 11 stitches and 15 rows make a 4-inch square on size 13 needles, before felting

### FINISHED MEASUREMENTS

» Size small fits 18- to 20-inch head circumference
» Size medium fits 20- to 22-inch head circumference
» Size large fits 22-inch and larger head circumference

### SKILLS & METHODS

» Felting
» Fringe
» I-cord
» Intarsia
» Stockinette stitch

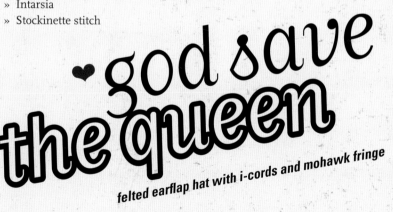

god save the queen

*felted earflap hat with i-cords and mohawk fringe*

*continued »*

Like our "Punk's Not Dead" hat, this is assembled out of 4 pieces. Although this version is intarsia-heavy and somewhat time-consuming, the finished piece makes it all worthwhile. First you will knit the 2 side pieces. Next you will pick up stitches at the bottom edge of each piece and knit the earflaps directly on, finishing with an I-cord on both. Then you will attach the 2 sides by sewing them together along the center seam. Finally, you will attach fringe to the end of each I-cord and 2 rows of fringe along the center seam, with colors corresponding to the flag design for the Mohawk.

To begin, prepare 4 balls of blue yarn, 6 balls of white yarn, and 3 balls of red yarn. Use yarn bobbins if you prefer, or just keep separate balls of yarn. Cast on 30 stitches in the following order: 3 blue, 2 white, 2 red, 1 white, 3 blue, 2 white, 5 red, 2 white, 3 blue, 1 white, 2 red, 1 white, and 3 blue on regular needles. This counts as the first row of the right intarsia graph. Work rows 2 to 24 in stockinette stitch, following the right intarsia graph. To create the rounded dome, you will only decrease along the side edges so as to retain the red cross in the center. When decreasing, we suggest knitting or purling the second and third stitches together as well as the second- and third-to-last stitches together to maintain a clean edge. Continue following the intarsia graph, decreasing at the beginning and end of rows 25, 27, 29, 30, 31, 32, 33, 34, 35, 36, 37, and 38; 6 stitches will remain. Bind off. Repeat to create second piece.

To create the earflaps, pick up 17 stitches on the bottom edge of the piece, starting at the sixth stitch for the right side of the hat. Following the right intarsia graph, the yarn color order will be 1 red, 2 white, 3 blue, 2 white, 5 red, 2 white, and 2 blue. For the left side of the hat, pick up 17 stitches across the bottom, starting at the 10th stitch. The yarn color order will be 2 blue, 2 white, 5 red, 2 white, 3 blue, 2 white, and 1 red. The following instruc-

tions apply to both earflaps: Following the intarsia graph, work 4 rows in stockinette stitch. Begin side edge decreases at the beginning and end of rows 5, 8, 11, 14, and 17. On row 20, the last row of your earflap, use the red yarn only. Knit the first 3 stitches together, knit the fourth stitch, and then knit the last 3 stitches together. You are left with 3 red stitches. Transfer your knitting to double-pointed needles to make the I-cord. Take the needle with the knitting in your left hand, and slide all the stitches to the right end of the needle. Pull the yarn from the left side of the work across the back, and knit the first right-hand stitch. Knit to the end. Slide your work to the right end of the needle, and repeat until the I-cord is approximately 12 inches long. Bind off.

Lay the 2 pieces together, right sides facing each other, and stitch together along the outer seam with your darning needle and a length of yarn, making sure the edges of the flag design line up. Weave all of the loose strands into the back of the knitting. Turn right-side out.

For the fringe, cut 6-inch strands of yarn according to the following instructions. Since the I-cords are solid red, we did the I-cord fringe in blue and white. You will need 2 sets of fringe, each comprising 3 strands of white yarn and 3 strands of blue yarn. See the glossary for tips on cutting and knotting fringe. Insert your crochet hook through 2 strands at the end of the I-cord. Hook, pull through, and knot 1 set of white and blue yarn. Repeat this step to attach fringe to the end of the second I-cord.

The difference between the Mohawk on this hat and our "Punk's Not Dead" is that it is a wee bit shorter and each fringe set varies in color and amount, corresponding to the overall flag design. Cut and lay out in order the following sets of 6-inch strands of yarn. You will need 2 sets of the following for the complete Mohawk (a total of 46 fringe sets, 23 on each side of the hat). To do this quickly and precisely, all you need is a 3-inch-by-3-inch piece of cardboard and a pair of scissors. Hold the yarn by its end at the bottom edge of the cardboard, and wrap it around the cardboard as many times as the number of strands outlined below. Snip horizontally across the bottom.

*set 1:* 10 blue strands
*set 2:* 10 blue strands
*set 3:* 6 white strands
*set 4:* 10 red strands
*set 5:* 6 white strands
*set 6:* 10 blue strands
*set 7:* 4 white strands
*set 8:* 5 red strands
*set 9:* 4 white strands
*set 10:* 10 blue strands
*set 11:* 6 white strands
*set 12:* 10 red strands

*set 13:* 6 white strands
*set 14:* 10 blue strands
*set 15:* 4 white strands
*set 16:* 5 red strands
*set 17:* 4 white strands
*set 18:* 10 blue strands
*set 19:* 6 white strands
*set 20:* 10 red strands
*set 21:* 6 white strands
*set 22:* 10 blue strands
*set 23:* 10 blue strands

Basically, you will attach 2 rows of fringe back-to-back on either side of the center seam in the order outlined above, corresponding to the flag pattern. For 1 side, insert your crochet hook through the first stitch next to the seam in the third row. Hook, pull through, and knot the first set. The fringe knot should face the right side of the fabric. Following along the center seam, attach each fringe set through the stitch next to the seam corresponding to the color of the flag design. You will end up with 23 fringe sets on this side. Flip the hat over, and repeat on the second side.

To felt, throw the finished hat into a washing machine wash on 1 hot cycle, without any detergent or conditioner. Remove the hat from the washing machine, and separate each I-cord fringe strand and each Mohawk fringe strand by grabbing 1 strand in each hand and tearing them apart, down to the knot. This will enhance the overall look of the Mohawk. ❤

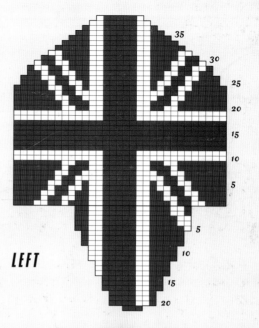

LEFT

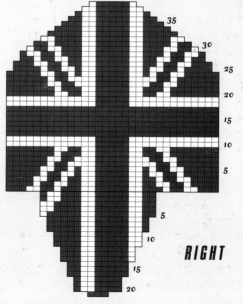

RIGHT

CHaPTer *o2*

FoR the

neck

*the brilliant colors of this scarf are a tribute to ska's jamaican roots. reggae beats were prevalent in music by many punk bands, including some of our favorites of all time, the clash and the police. we did this scarf in a garter stitch so the finished project won't curl up.*

### MATERIALS
» 32-inch size 8 circular needle, or size required to get correct gauge
» Row counter, optional
» Darning needle
» 1 skein orange cotton/silk blend worsted-weight yarn (Noro Lily, 70% cotton, 30% silk, #13)
» 1 skein lime green cotton/silk blend worsted-weight yarn (Noro Lily, 70% cotton, 30% silk, #7)
» 1 skein olive green cotton/silk blend worsted-weight yarn (Noro Lily, 70% cotton, 30% silk, #6)
» 1 skein yellow cotton/silk blend worsted-weight yarn (Noro Lily, 70% cotton, 30% silk, #8)

### GAUGE (IN GARTER STITCH)
» 14 stitches and 40 rows make a 4-inch square

### FINISHED MEASUREMENTS
» Approximately 86 inches by 4 inches

### SKILLS & METHODS
» Garter stitch

ska
skarf ♥

horizontal multistriped garter-stitch scarf

Cast on 300 stitches in orange. Knit 5 rows. Cut off orange yarn, leaving a 3-inch strand. (Do this at every color switch.) Switch to lime green yarn, and knit 3 rows. Switch to olive green yarn, and knit 5 rows. Switch to yellow yarn, and knit 9 rows. Switch to orange yarn, and knit 3 rows. Switch to olive green yarn, and knit 3 rows. Switch to lime green yarn, and knit 5 rows. Switch to olive green yarn, and knit 1 row. Switch to yellow yarn, and knit 3 rows. Finally, switch to orange, and knit 1 row. Bind off. Use a darning needle to weave in all loose ends. ♥

ac/dc's angus young showed that school uniforms aren't just for school. this red tie adds a spot of color and sophistication to any outfit. customize it with pins of your favorite punk band logos, kilt pins, or other dramatic hardware.

## MATERIALS

» Size 5 needles, or size required to get correct gauge
» Row counter, optional
» Size 0 crochet hook
» Darning needle
» 1 skein dark red worsted-weight wool yarn (Cascade 220, 100% Peruvian Highland wool, Ruby, #9404)

## GAUGE (IN STOCKINETTE STITCH)

» 24 stitches and 32 rows make a 4-inch square

## FINISHED MEASUREMENTS

» $37^3/_4$ inches by $2^1/_2$ inches at the widest part, and $1^1/_4$ inches at the narrowest part before crocheted edge and blocking; 46 inches by $3^1/_4$ inches at the widest part, and $1^1/_2$ inches at the narrowest part after crocheted edge and blocking

## SKILLS & METHODS

» Crochet (single)
» Stockinette stitch
» Felting

moral panic

schoolboy tie

*continued »*

pretty *in* PuNk

For this project, you will begin at the widest section of the tie. You will work in stockinette stitch for 286 rows (approximately 36 inches), making 8 sets of decreases along the way. Then you will pick up stitches on your cast-on row and knit the bottom triangle. Finally, you will finish with a single crocheted edge all around the perimeter of the tie.

Cast on 16 stitches. Work in stockinette stitch for 23 rows. You will then repeat a pattern of decrease rows throughout this pattern, where you knit or purl together the second and third stitches on the row as well as the second- and third-to-last stitches. Work these decrease rows on rows 24, 48, 72, and 96, while continuing to work stockinette stitch on all other rows. You will have 8 stitches remaining. Work rows 97 through 280 in stockinette stitch. If you're not interested in counting from here on, that is about 24 inches after your last decrease row. On row 281, or 24 inches after decrease rows, you will work a decrease row again in order to shape the triangular end of the tie. Work decrease rows every other row until 2 stitches remain. Knit or purl these last 2 stitches together. Cut the end of the yarn, and pull through the remaining stitch.

Finally, you will make the triangular shaping for the widest part of your tie. Simply pick up 16 stitches along your cast-on row. Then work decrease rows every other row until 2 stitches remain. Knit together your final 2 stitches, cut the yarn, and pull the end through remaining stitch.

For the trim, single crochet into every other stitch along the entire perimeter of the tie, beginning at the tip of the narrow triangular end. Use your darning needle to weave the loose threads into the back of the knitting.

To even out the stitches and lightly felt, agitate and massage the piece in alternating baths of cold water and hot water with conditioner, 3 times. Wring out and roll in a towel to remove excess moisture. Pin flat and let dry overnight. Press with a hot iron. ❤

*as huge fans of vampire films, we got the idea for this scarf when we found the perfect blood-red yarn. unfortunately, the store only had one skein. we figured it was enough for a dramatically long and skinny scarf, but it turned out that some stretching and pulling were necessary to get it just right. the crocheted lace scalloped edge really adds a gothic flair.*

## vamp
long, thin garter-stitch scarf
with crocheted scalloped edge

### MATERIALS
» Size 15 needles, or size required to get correct gauge
» Size J crochet hook
» Row counter, optional
» Darning needle
» 1 skein red alpaca bulky-weight yarn (Baby Alpaca Grande, 100% baby alpaca, Red, #2050)
» 1 skein black mohair worsted-weight yarn (Joseph Galler Yarns, Flore II, 75% kid mohair, 20% wool, 5% nylon, #015)

### GAUGE (IN GARTER STITCH)
» 8 stitches and 8 rows make a 4-inch square (before stretching)

### FINISHED MEASUREMENTS
» 79 inches by $3^{1}/_{2}$ inches after stretching

### SKILLS & METHODS
» Crochet (single, double, triple)
» Garter stitch

*continued »*

Cast on 10 stitches. Slip the first stitch of each row. This creates a neater edge along the sides and will be important when you crochet the lace edging. Knit 75 rows in garter stitch (or until you run out of yarn). You will have a short and boring scarf. Do not despair...

For this scarf, rinse in a cold water and conditioner bath, and wring out. You don't have to be too careful since you will now stretch it out. Pull the scarf lengthwise with some force. You are essentially taking the garter stitches apart, without unraveling.

Your scarf should now be almost twice as long and narrow. Place flat on a towel (no need to block), and let it dry completely.

Work edging using a crochet hook and the black mohair. Single crochet the black mohair once in each slipped edge stitch, once in each cast-on stitch, and once in each bind-off stitch all around the perimeter of the scarf. Chain through the first stitch to join the round. On the next round you will create the scallop as follows: single crochet into the first single crochet, double crochet into the next single crochet, triple crochet into the third single crochet, chain 3, slip stitch into the triple crochet just created, double crochet into the fourth single crochet, single crochet into the fifth single crochet, slip stitch into the next 2 single crochets (numbers 6 and 7), and begin this 7-stitch pattern all over again. Join with a final slip stitch to the first single crochet of the pattern. ❤

we designed this bold checkerboard scarf as a nod to our favorite ska bands of the 2-tone era. growing up in the '80s, spending endless hours watching music videos, we were drawn to the distinct and sharp style of the specials, the english beat, and madness.

## MATERIALS

- » Size 7 knitting needles, or size required to get correct gauge
- » Yarn bobbins, optional
- » Row counter, optional
- » Darning needle
- » 2 red buttons (approximately $7/8$-inch in diameter)
- » 1 skein black DK/light worsted-weight yarn (Rowan Cashsoft DK, 57% extrafine merino, 33% microfiber, 10% cashmere, Black, #519)
- » 1 skein white DK/light worsted-weight yarn (Rowan Cashsoft DK, 57% extrafine merino, 33% microfiber, 10% cashmere, Baby Snowman, #800)

## GAUGE (IN STOCKINETTE STITCH)

- » 20 stitches and 30 rows make a 4-inch square

## FINISHED MEASUREMENTS

- » 14 inches by $2^1/4$ inches

## SKILLS & METHODS

- » Intarsia
- » Stockinette stitch

## rude girl

checkerboard choker with red button detail

continued »

pretty in PuNk

This is a quick knit, but taking some extra time for prepping and finishing is well worth the effort. The choker is knit horizontally, even though this may seem counterintuitive. Having tried to do it both ways, we found this method to be a much cleaner and neater knit than vertically.

Begin by preparing 6 balls or yarn bobbins of black yarn with approximately 6 yards of yarn on each. (This is approximately 5 generous arm's lengths of yarn for each ball, if you're not interested in measuring.) Do the same with the white yarn.

Begin your cast-on row as follows: using the double cast-on method (also known as the continental or long-tail method), cast on 8 stitches in white, then 8 stitches in black, and continue in that alternating pattern, using a separate ball of yarn for each set, until you have 9 sets of 8 stitches in alternating black and white. Work in stockinette stitch, interlocking the black and white yarns wherever they meet, as you would for any intarsia knitting. On the fourth row, in the first checkerboard square, which should be white, you will begin to create a buttonhole. This is very simple to do. After knitting 4 of the 8 stitches of this white square, take a new ball of white yarn, and knit the last 4 stitches using the newest white yarn without interlocking the yarns as you normally would with intarsia. Do this for the next 2 rows as well. Then, on row 7, close off the buttonhole by using only 1 white ball for that

square again. Continue until 11 rows have been worked. You will just have finished purling that row.

At this point, transfer all 72 stitches from 1 needle to another, so that you can purl a row again without getting out of the stockinette stitch pattern. The checkerboard effect of the design now comes to play. Wherever there was a white square, you will begin a black one and vice versa. The simplest way to achieve this without too much fuss is to take a new black ball of yarn and begin purling. When you reach the second square, which is now to be white, you will conveniently have the white yarn from the previous purled row ready to use via the intarsia method.

This time around, you will begin to make your second buttonhole on the fifth row of the first checkerboard square, which should be black this time. The reason you do this on the fifth row of knitting instead of the fourth is that the original cast-on row needs to be taken into consideration. The buttonhole is done the same way as last time; simply use a new ball of black yarn, and then on the eighth row, close off the buttonhole by using 1 ball of black again.

The last complicated bit comes during the bind-off. After 10 rows are worked, you will bind off on the purl row. Begin binding off in purling as you usually would, but remember to change to the next color of yarn 1 stitch before the end of the block. That way, when you bind off the first stitch of a new color block, you will have the correct yarn color on the needle.

After binding off all stitches, take all the necessary time needed to weave in all loose yarn using a darning needle. Be especially careful around the buttonholes, where you will have several dangling threads of yarn.

Finally, rinse the finished choker in a cold water and conditioner bath. Dry the choker carefully by rolling it in a towel, and block the piece to dry perfectly straight. After it is dry, sew on your red buttons. ❤

CHaPTer o3

for The

# chest

*every day is halloween when you wear this cobweb-inspired jumper. wear it over a colorful camisole for a sexy look, or over graphic t-shirts to add texture to your punk-rock ensemble.*

# goth girl
### loose-knit tight-fit holey jumper

## MATERIALS
» 16-inch size 17 circular needle, or size required to get correct gauge
» 2 stitch holders
» 1 skein black fingering-weight mohair yarn (Karabella Gossamer, 52% nylon, 30% kid mohair, 18% polyester, Black with Black, #6800)

## GAUGE [IN STOCKINETTE STITCH]
» 7 stitches and 9 rows make a 4-inch square

## FINISHED MEASUREMENTS [SIZES MEDIUM AND LARGE ARE GIVEN IN PARENTHESES]
» This project appears small when finished, but will stretch and conform to the body like a stocking. Small fits a 32-34 inch bust; medium a 34-36 inch bust; and large a 36-38 inch bust.

## SKILLS & METHODS
» Dropped stitch
» Knitting in the round
» Stockinette stitch
» Yarn over

*continued »*

This sweater is knit completely in the round in stockinette stitch so that there are no seams to break up the sheer spiderweb lace look achieved from knitting the fine yarn on such oversize needles. You will essentially be knitting 1 large tube for the body of the sweater and 2 smaller tubes for the sleeves. A dropped stitch and a few yarn overs add to the overall distressed look!

Begin by casting on 50 (58, 66) stitches, and join the beginning and end of the round, being careful not to twist the cast-on row. Work in stockinette stitch, knitting every round, until you reach 18 (20, 22) inches. This is the body of the sweater up to the underarm. At this point, transfer 40 (48, 56) of the stitches onto 2 stitch holders, and keep 10 stitches on your needles to begin 1 sleeve. In addition to the 10 stitches, cast on another 10 (14, 18) stitches. Join the beginning and end of the round, being careful not to twist the new cast-on row, and work these 20 (24, 28)

stitches circularly in stockinette stitch. At random points, place 1 or 2 yarn overs that will develop into holes. Bind off when the sleeve measures 24 (25, 26) inches.

Before making the second sleeve, drop a stitch about 2 stitches away from the first sleeve. Let the dropped stitch run all the way down the body of the sweater to create a ladder effect. To make the second sleeve, keep 15 (19, 23) stitches on each side of the first sleeve (including the 1 dropped stitch) on stitch holders, and use the remaining 10 stitches opposite the first sleeve to begin. In addition to these 10 stitches, cast on another 10 (14, 18) stitches, and repeat as for the first sleeve.

At this point, pick up all of the live stitches from your stitch holders and also pick up stitches from your sleeve cast-on row; you should pick up a total of 50 (66, 82) stitches. Knit 2 rounds. After the 2 rounds, place markers around each of the 10 (14, 18) stitches that comprise the outside of the sleeves. On the third round, knit 2 together 5 (7, 9) times along each of the 10 (14, 18) stitches you marked. At the end of this row, you will have 40 (52, 64) stitches total and a somewhat narrower neckline. Knit 2 more rounds and bind off. ♥

*for an everyday dominatrix look, we created a simple tube top but added ingeniously placed faux runs, dropped stitches, and bra straps. to add to the overall sexiness, use an incredibly soft and luxurious cashmere. it not only looks great but also feels sensuous next to your skin.*

## master & servant
camisole with dropped stitches and bra straps

### MATERIALS
- » Size 7 straight needles, or size required to get correct gauge
- » Stitch markers
- » Darning needle
- » 1 set of old bra straps
- » 2 skeins black worsted-weight yarn (Rowan Cashsoft Aran, 57% extra-fine merino, 33% microfiber, 10% cashmere, Black, #11)

### GAUGE (IN STOCKINETTE STITCH)
- » 17 stitches and 24 rows make a 4-inch square

### FINISHED MEASUREMENTS (SIZES MEDIUM AND LARGE ARE GIVEN IN PARENTHESES)
- » 27 (30, 33) inches by 11 (12, 13) inches

### SKILLS & METHODS
- » Stockinette stitch
- » Yarn over

*continued »*

This sexy little top is constructed from an easy knitted wide rectangle with some smartly placed yarn overs and runs that create curvy body shaping. A simple center back seam joins the rectangle into a tube top, then bra straps are sewn on to make it into a camisole.

The camisole is knit from the top down. Using the single-yarn method, cast on a total of 108 (126, 138) stitches as follows: cast on 54 (63, 69), make a triple yarn over, then cast on 54 (63, 69) more stitches. The 3 loops of the yarn over will begin the V-ladder featured on the front center of the camisole. On the first row, purl 54 (63, 69) stitches, drop the triple yarn over loops, make another triple yarn over, and purl the remaining 54 (63, 69) stitches. Repeat this again for the second row. Knit the third row, and continue to work from now on in stockinette stitch. Continue to make a triple yarn over in the center for the next 3 rows, dropping them to make the ladders and adding new ones each time. After 6 sets, you will continue in stockinette stitch and make 8 rows with double yarn overs. Following the 8 rows of double yarn

overs, make 10 rows of single yarn overs. This will have an overall effect of a V-shaped ladder of dropped stitches.

Work in stockinette stitch until the top measures $8^{1}/_{2}$ ($9^{1}/_{2}$, $10^{1}/_{2}$) inches from the beginning. Place markers after the 37th (43rd, 47th) stitch and after the 71st (83rd, 91st) stitch. This marks where the next sets of yarn-over ladders will be placed. Continue to work in stockinette while making the following sets of yarn overs and dropping them on the next row. Work 7 rows with single yarn overs at the stitch markers, then 5 rows with double yarn overs. Purl the next row, while maintaining the double yarn overs at the markers. Bind off in purling, and again continue to maintain the double yarn overs. At the same time, you will also drop stitches on purpose just before binding off. You will drop stitch number 3 (3, 3), 29 (34, 37), 79 (92, 101), and 106 (124, 136) and let the ladder of dropped stitches work all the way up to the top of the camisole.

Use mattress stitch to seam up the back of the top. Then sew on the bra straps about 14 (16, 18) stitches to the left and right of the center in the front and the back. This camisole looks best when it is rinsed in a conditioner bath and blocked until completely dry. ❤

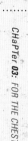

bulky knits don't have to leave you looking shapeless. a few alterations to a simple classic style can turn the ordinary into extraordinary. the detached and removable sleeves in this halter-neck jumper offer a sexy glimpse of exposed shoulders. the bold cross design on the jumper adds a flattering focal point, and if worn as a minidress, it is sinfully salty!

## MATERIALS

» 32-inch size 17 circular needle, or size required to get correct gauge
» Stitch markers
» 3 stitch holders
» Darning needle
» Size 17 straight needles, optional
» 6 skeins black superbulky yarn (Blue Sky Bulky, 50% alpaca, 50% merino wool, Black Bear, #1008)
» 2 skeins blue superbulky yarn (Blue Sky Bulky, 50% alpaca, 50% merino wool, Dark Blue, #1013)

## GAUGE (IN STOCKINETTE STITCH)

» $7^{1}/_{4}$ stitches and 11 rows make a 4-inch square

## FINISHED MEASUREMENTS

» See body and sleeve illustrations

## SKILLS & METHODS

» Intarsia
» Stockinette stitch

# transgression

superbulky jumper with cross design and detached sleeves

continued »

*pretty in PuNk*

This sweater is worked in stockinette stitch throughout on circular needles but not knit in the round. The detached sleeves are also knit in stockinette stitch throughout. The only seams are in the center of the back of the sweater and up the sleeves.

Using 2 balls of black and 1 ball of blue, take the circular needle and cast on 60 stitches as follows: 27 in black, 6 in blue, and another 27 in black. Work in stockinette stitch, using intarsia to keep the center 6 stitches blue to create the vertical line of the cross until the body of the sweater measures 13 1/2 inches; this should be 36 rows. Place 2 stitch markers around the center 30 stitches (after 15 stitches and 45 stitches) to mark the area where the horizontal blue stripe of the cross will be. Cut the blue yarn, and join again at the first marker when knitting the next row. Work 8 rows using intarsia to keep the stitches between the markers blue.

At this point transfer each set of black stitches (15 each) onto stitch holders or the straight needles, reserve for the back of the sweater, and remove the stitch markers. You will now be creating the front of the sweater, shaping the armholes and continuing the vertical line of the blue cross in intarsia with the 30 stitches on your needles. Reintroducing the 2 balls of black yarn and the center 6 in blue, work in stockinette stitch for the next 14 rows while simultaneously decreasing a stitch at the beginning of every row. Knit together the second and third stitches of each row in order to keep a neat edge. This will result in an overall decrease of 7 stitches on each side; 16 stitches remain on your needle. Work 4 more rows in stockinette, maintaining the top of the blue cross in intarsia without any further decreases. Transfer these 16 stitches onto a stitch holder, and commence work on the back armholes.

Transfer the back stitches from their holders onto your needle. For the back armholes, you will be working across all 30 stitches with only 1 ball of black yarn. Work in stockinette stitch for the next 14 rows while decreasing at the beginning of every row. Remember to knit together the second and third stitches of each row in order to keep a neat edge. This will result in an overall decrease of 7 stitches on each side; 16 stitches remain. Then work 4 more rows in stockinette without any further decreases. At this point transfer the 16 stitches for the front onto the circular needle, so there are 32 stitches in all. Work in stockinette stitch for 6 rows, continuing to use intarsia for the center 6 stitches in blue and using 2 balls of black yarn. Bind off. Remember, during this color changing, bind off to introduce the blue color 1 stitch before the intarsia pattern begins on the bind-off row, so that when you slip the stitch during bind-off, the pattern is maintained. Do this again when introducing the second ball of black.

The sweater is almost finished. You will notice 2 slits along the back. One is a small 2-inch slit at the neck, which you can seam together simply with a darning needle and black yarn. The second slit is in the center back, below the armhole. To seam this together, we used the contrasting blue superbulky alpaca, using about 2 yards to crisscross a seam, much as you do when lacing shoes. This creates a decorative blue braid. We double-knotted the end and left a few inches hanging for a messy look.

One sleeve will have a blue stripe at the widest point, while the other sleeve will have a blue stripe at the narrowest point. For the first sleeve, cast on 18 stitches in blue, and work 7 rows even. Knit 2 together at the beginning of the seventh row; you will have 17 stitches left. Switch to the black yarn, work stockinette stitch, and knit 2 together at the beginning of rows 13, 19, 25, 31, 37, and 43.

## BODY

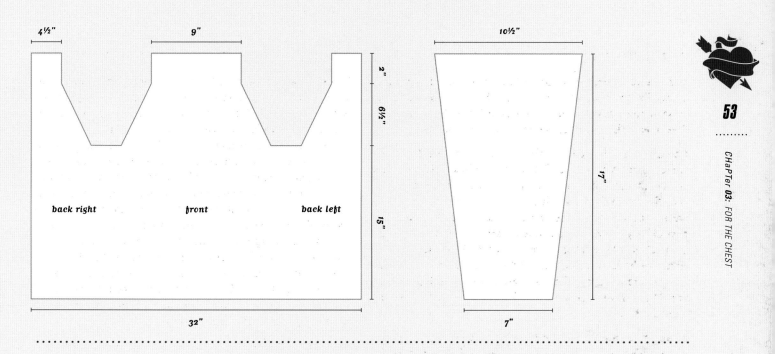

**4½"**  **9"**

back right    front    back left

**32"**

## SLEEVE

**10½"**

**2"**

**6½"**

**17"**

**15"**

**7"**

You will have 11 stitches remaining. Knit 1 row, and then bind off.

For the second sleeve, cast on 18 stitches with the black yarn. Make decreases by knitting 2 together at the end of the row on rows 7, 13, 19, 25, and 31. Continue working even in stockinette stitch in black, switching to blue yarn on the 37th row. Knit 2 together in blue at the end of this row and again on the 43rd row. You will have 11 stitches remaining. Knit 1 more row in blue, and bind off.

Use the same technique as the back of the sweater to seam together the sleeves. Take about 2 yards of the bulky alpaca, and lace the sleeves as you would shoes. Double-knot and leave a tail for decoration.

This superbulky yarn has a very soft and fuzzy texture and blooms beautifully when it is knit. It requires no washing, conditioning, or blocking.

Please note that the sweater is shown photographed on a petite model. If you are interested in making a minidress out of yours, take some extra time. Measure from your underarm to the desired length of the minidress, and make sure to lengthen the sweater accordingly. You can keep all armhole shaping, neck shaping, and detached sleeves the same. Note that this will require more yarn! ❤

*no punk-rock wardrobe is complete without the quintessential over-sized striped mohair sweater worn by many famous punk rockers in the late 1970s. for the past 10 years, whenever we found ourselves in a yarn store looking at the mohair collection, we would inevitably say, "we have to make that sweater one of these days!" and now we finally have! we chose an acerbic green-and-black color palette for ours, but feel free to pair your two favorite colors.*

## MATERIALS

» Size 11 knitting needles, or size required to get correct gauge
» Row counter, optional
» 4 stitch holders
» Darning needle
» 3 skeins black worsted-weight mohair yarn (Joseph Galler Yarns, Flore II, 75% kid mohair, 20% wool, 5% nylon, Black, #015)
» 3 skeins green worsted-weight mohair yarn (Joseph Galler Yarns, Flore II, 75% kid mohair, 20% wool, 5% nylon, Lime, #104)

## GAUGE [IN STOCKINETTE STITCH]

» 12 stitches and 16 rows make a 4-inch square on size 11 needles

## the swindle
boxy striped jumper

## FINISHED MEASUREMENTS

» See front & back and sleeve illustrations

## SKILLS & METHODS

» Stockinette stitch
» 3-needle bind-off

*continued »*

We intentionally designed this sweater to be large and comfy. It is made up of 4 pieces: identical front and back pieces and 2 sleeves.

For the front, cast on 57 stitches in black mohair. Work 64 rows in stockinette stitch, alternating every 16 rows between black mohair and green mohair.

To shape the armholes, switch to the black mohair, and work the next few rows in stockinette stitch according to the following directions. Bind off the first 2 stitches at the beginning of the next 4 rows. Then work decreases at the beginning and end of your row by knitting 2 together on the next 2 knit rows. You should have worked 71 rows and have 45 stitches remaining at this point.

Work through row 90 in stockinette stitch, switching colors every 16 rows as before. Begin the neck hole shaping on row 91 by knitting the first 12 stitches, binding off the center 21 stitches, and knitting the last 12 stitches. Note that the stitches for the left shoulder will remain on the far end of your needle but will not be worked until later. Continue working just the right shoulder as follows:

*row 92:* Purl.
*row 93:* Bind off the first 3 stitches at the neck opening, and knit to the end; 9 stitches remain.
*row 94:* Purl.
*row 95:* Bind off the first stitch at the neck opening, and knit to the end; 8 stitches remain.
*row 96:* Purl.

Do not bind off. Transfer the remaining 8 stitches to a stitch holder because you will join the pieces together at the shoulders with a 3-needle bind-off.

For the left side, slip stitches to the other needle. Attach green mohair at the shoulder edge, and work in stockinette stitch as follows:

*row 92:* Knit.
*row 93:* Bind off the first 3 stitches at the neck opening, and purl to the end; 9 stitches will remain.
*row 94:* Knit.
*row 95:* Bind off the first stitch at the neck opening, and purl to the end; 8 stitches will remain.
*row 96:* Knit.

Again, do not bind off. Transfer the remaining 8 stitches to a stitch holder for a 3-needle bind-off seam. Repeat to create the back piece.

To attach the front and back pieces at the shoulders, place both pieces together, right sides facing each other, and join each shoulder with a 3-needle bind-off (see instructions in glossary).

To create the sleeves, cast on 24 stitches in green mohair. Work 80 rows in stockinette stitch, alternating every 16 rows between green mohair and black mohair. Note: you will increase 1 stitch at the beginning and end of rows 13, 26, 39, 52, 65, and 78. You will now have 36 stitches. Switch back to black mohair, and begin shaping the cap of the sleeve by binding off the first 2 stitches of the next 4 rows. Then work decreases at the beginning and end of your row by knitting 2 together on the next 2 knit rows.

## FRONT & BACK

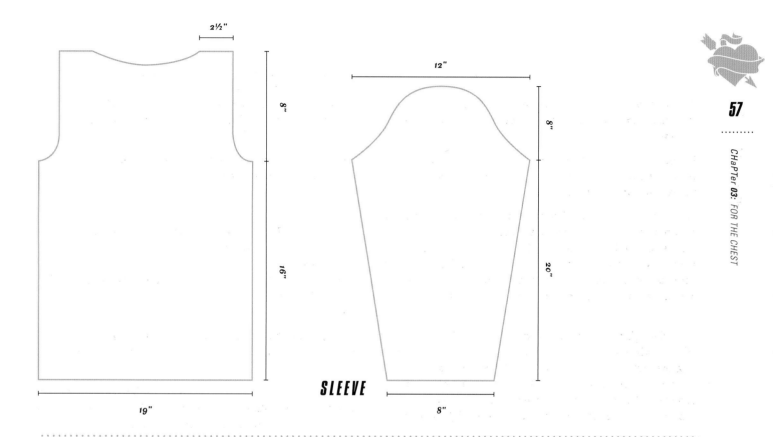

2½"

8"

16"

19"

**SLEEVE**

12"

8"

20"

8"

You should have worked 87 rows with 24 stitches remaining at this point. Work rows 88 through 96 in stockinette stitch. Switch to green mohair, and work rows 97 through 109 in stockinette stitch, knitting together the second and third stitches as well as the second- and third-to-last stitches on rows 99, 101, 103, 105, 107, and 109; 12 stitches remain. On row 110, purl together the second and third stitches as well as the second- and third-to-last

stitches; 10 stitches remain. On row 111, knit together the second and third stitches, the fourth and fifth stitches, the sixth and seventh stitches, and the eighth and ninth stitches. Bind off the remaining 6 stitches. Repeat to create the second sleeve.

Using a 1-stitch seam allowance, set in sleeves and sew to armhole edges. Finally, sew the side seams and the sleeve seams. 🖤

*in keeping with the schoolboy theme, here is a conventional sweater vest with a nautical twist. nineteen-fifties pinup girls were often dressed thematically, and we chose the sailor motif for our look, customizing with an anchor patch and buttons.*

# the young one

sweater vest with nautical details

## MATERIALS
» Size 8 knitting needles, or size required to get correct gauge
» Row counter, optional
» 4 stitch holders
» 24-inch size 8 circular needle
» Darning needle
» Patch, optional
» 5 buttons, optional

» 5 skeins blue cotton fleece worsted-weight yarn (Brown Sheep Co., Lamb's Pride, Cotton Fleece, 80% cotton, 20% merino wool, Wolverine Blue, CW585)

## GAUGE (IN STOCKINETTE STITCH)
» 16 stitches and 24 rows make a 4-inch square

## FINISHED MEASUREMENTS
## (SIZES MEDIUM AND LARGE GIVEN IN PARENTHESES)
» See front and back illustrations

## SKILLS & METHODS
» Ribbing
» Stockinette stitch
» 3-needle bind-off

*continued »*

This vest is made up of 2 pieces: a front piece and a back piece. Ribbing is added to the armholes and V-neck. Finally, we added a personal touch with an iron-on patch and decorative buttons.

This project is worked with 2 strands of yarn held together throughout. For the front piece, cast on 64 (72, 80) stitches. To create the bottom ribbed edge, knit 4 stitches, then purl 4 stitches, alternating to the end of the row. Work in ribbing for 8 rows. Work rows 9 through 72 (76, 78) in stockinette stitch. Your piece should measure approximately 12 (12 1/2, 13) inches long.

At this point you will divide the piece in half, working the V-neck and armhole decreases first for the right side and then for the left side. Keep the first 32 (36, 40) stitches on your left needle, and transfer the last 32 (36, 40) stitches onto a stitch holder. For the left side, shape the left armhole and V-neck as follows:

*row 73 (77, 79):* Bind off the first 2 stitches, and knit to the end; 30 (34, 38) stitches remain.
*row 74 (78, 80):* Purl 1, purl together the second and third stitches, and purl to the end; 29 (33, 37) stitches remain.
*row 75 (79, 81):* Bind off the first 2 stitches, and knit to the end; 27 (31, 35) stitches remain.
*row 76 (80, 82):* Purl.
*row 77 (81, 83):* Bind off the first stitch, and knit to the end; 26 (30, 34) stitches remain.
*row 78 (82, 84):* Purl.
*row 79 (83, 85):* Bind off the first stitch, and knit to the end; 25 (29, 33) stitches remain.
*row 80 (84, 86):* Purl 1, purl together the second and third stitches, and purl to the end; 24 (28, 32) stitches remain.

*row 81 (85, 87):* Bind off the first stitch, and knit to the end; 23 (27, 31) stitches remain. This concludes the right armhole shaping.

To finish the V-neck, work rows 82 (86, 88) through 126 (130, 132) in stockinette stitch, purling together the second and third stitches on rows 86 (90, 92), 90 (94, 96), 94 (98, 100), 98 (102, 104), 102 (106, 108), 106 (110, 112), 110 (114, 116), 114 (118, 120), 118 (122, 124), 122 (126, 128), and 126 (130, 132). For the small size, transfer the remaining 12 stitches onto a stitch holder because you will join the front and back pieces together at the shoulders with a 3-needle bind-off. For the medium size, continue working in stockinette stitch for another 3 rows, then transfer the remaining 16 stitches onto a stitch holder. For the large size, continue working in stockinette stitch for another 6 rows, then transfer the remaining 20 stitches onto a stitch holder.

For the right side, transfer 32 (36, 40) stitches from the stitch holder onto your needle. Attach 2 strands of blue yarn at the armhole edge, and shape the right armhole and V-neck as follows:

*row 73 (77, 79) (wrong side):* Bind off the first 2 stitches, and purl to the end; 30 (34, 38) stitches remain.
*row 74 (78, 80) (right side):* Knit 1, knit together the second and third stitches, and knit to the end; 29 (33, 37) stitches remain.
*row 75 (79, 81):* Bind off the first 2 stitches, and purl to the end; 27 (31, 35) stitches remain.
*row 76 (80, 82):* Knit.
*row 77 (81, 83):* Bind off the first stitch, and purl to the end; 26 (30, 34) stitches remain.
*row 78 (82, 84):* Knit.

**FRONT**

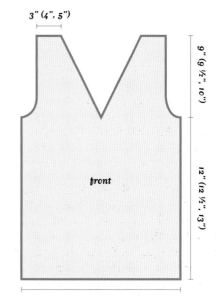

3" (4", 5")

9" (9½", 10")

12" (12½", 13")

front

16" (18", 20")

**BACK**

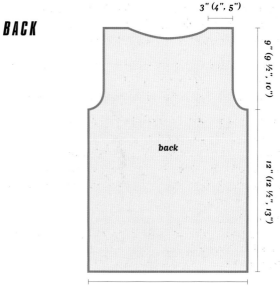

3" (4", 5")

9" (9½", 10")

12" (12½", 13")

back

16" (18", 20")

*row 79 (83, 85):* Bind off the first stitch, and purl to the end; 25 (29, 33) stitches remain.

*row 80 (84, 86):* Knit 1, knit together the second and third stitches, and knit to the end; 24 (28, 32) stitches remain.

*row 81 (85, 87):* Bind off the first stitch, and purl to the end; 23 (27, 31) stitches remain. This concludes the left armhole shaping.

To finish the V-neck, work rows 82 (86, 88) through 126 (130, 132) in stockinette stitch, knitting together the second and third stitches on rows 86 (90, 92), 90 (94, 96), 94 (98, 100), 98 (102, 104), 102 (106, 108), 106 (110, 112), 110 (114, 116), 114 (118, 120), 118 (122, 124), 122 (126, 128), and 126 (130, 132). For the small size, transfer the remaining 12 stitches onto a stitch holder because you will join the front and back pieces together at the shoulders with a 3-needle bind-off. For the medium size, continue working in stockinette stitch for another 3 rows, then transfer the remaining 16 stitches onto a stitch holder. For the large size, continue working in stockinette stitch for another 6 rows, then transfer the remaining 20 stitches onto a stitch holder.

For the back piece, follow the instructions for the front up to and including row 72 (76, 78). Next, you will work both the right and left armholes at the same time as follows: At the beginning of the next 4 rows, bind off the first 2 stitches, and knit or purl to the end; 56 (64, 72) stitches remain. At the beginning of the next 6 rows, bind off the first stitch, and knit or purl to the end; 50 (58, 66) stitches remain. Work rows 83 (87, 89) through 120 (124, 126) even in stockinette stitch. On row 121 (125, 127), you will begin shaping the back neck opening. Knit the first 16 (20, 24) stitches, bind off the center 18 stitches, and then knit the

*continued »*

remaining 16 (20, 24) stitches. Transfer the first 16 (20, 24) stitches to a stitch holder so you can work the next 5 rows of the left side in stockinette stitch, binding off the first 2 stitches on every knit row. For the small size, transfer the remaining 12 stitches onto a stitch holder because you will join the front and back pieces together at the shoulders with a 3-needle bind-off. For the medium size, continue working in stockinette stitch for another 3 rows, then transfer the remaining 16 stitches onto a stitch holder. For the large size, continue working in stockinette stitch for another 6 rows, then transfer the remaining 20 stitches onto a stitch holder.

For the right side, transfer the 16 (20, 24) stitches back onto your knitting needle, purlwise. Attach 2 strands of blue yarn at the armhole edge, and work the next 5 rows in stockinette, binding off the first 2 stitches on every purl row. Leave these 12 (16, 20) stitches on your needle for the final 3-needle bind-off. For the small size, leave these remaining 12 stitches on a stitch holder because you will join the front and back pieces together at the shoulders with a 3-needle bind-off. For the medium size, continue working in stockinette stitch for another 3 rows, then leave the remaining 16 stitches on your needle for bind-off. For the large size, continue working in stockinette stitch for another 6 rows, then leave the remaining 20 stitches on your needle for bind-off.

To seam the shoulders, place the front and back pieces together, right sides facing each other, and join the top shoulder seams together using the 3-needle bind-off method.

To add ribbing to the V-neck opening, use a circular needle. Pick up 84 (90, 96) stitches around the perimeter of the neck opening, starting 1 stitch to the right of the center of the V-neck. You should pick up 30 (33, 36) stitches along the right side, 24 across the back of the neck, and 30 (33, 36) down the left side. When you are finished picking up, turn and work your first row on the wrong side. Knit 4 stitches, then purl 4 stitches, alternating to the end of the row. Turn and work across on the right side, working purl 4 stitches, then knit 4 stitches, alternating to the end of the row. Repeat these 2 rows for a total of 8 rows. Bind off in the corresponding knit 4, purl 4 pattern. To finish, stitch down the left side edge to the right side. Lay the right side edge over the left side ribbing, and stitch down.

To add ribbing to the right armhole, pick up 60 (66, 72) stitches along the edge of the armhole using the circular needle. Instead of the 8 rows you worked on the bottom and neck edge, you will work 4 rows of knit 4, purl 4, alternating across the row. Bind off in the corresponding knit 4, purl 4 pattern. Repeat on the left armhole. Using a 1-stitch seam allowance stitch, sew the side seams together using the darning needle. Weave all loose ends into the back of the knitting.

To add a personal touch, we ironed on an anchor patch and sewed 5 anchor-themed buttons down the right side seam. Feel free to customize as you like! ❤

one of the newest subgenres of punk-rock fashion is the "gothic lolita" style popular in japan today. this corset is knit in antique rose and accented in black, with a silk ribbon to emulate the clothing worn by victorian porcelain dolls. even if you are not a follower of the trend, this accessory can be worn over a simple tank top and jeans to spice up your outfit.

## MATERIALS

» Size 10¹/₂ straight needles, or size required to get correct gauge
» Darning needle
» Size G crochet hook
» 1 skein pink bulky-weight wool yarn (Brown Sheep Co., Lamb's Pride Bulky, 85% wool, 15% mohair, Lotus Pink, M38)
» 1 skein black bulky-weight wool yarn (Brown Sheep Co., Lamb's Pride Bulky, 85% wool, 15% mohair, Onyx, M05)
» 3¹/₄ yards of taupe colored silk ribbon, or ribbon of your choice, about 1¹/₂ inches wide

## GAUGE (IN STOCKINETTE STITCH)

» 15 stitches and 20 rows make a 4-inch square in ribbed pattern

## FINISHED MEASUREMENTS (SIZES MEDIUM AND LARGE ARE GIVEN IN PARENTHESES)

» 23 inches by 9 inches for small (when stretched)
» 25 inches by 10 inches for medium (when stretched)
» 27 inches by 11 inches for large (when stretched)

# lolita

vertical-striped ribbed corset with stitch and ribbon lacing detail

## SKILLS & METHODS

» Crochet (single)
» Duplicate stitch
» Intarsia
» Ribbing
» Stockinette stitch

continued »

This corset knits pretty quickly, but it's one of those projects where some preparation is worth the effort. You will be knitting a ribbed pattern while working vertical stripes of pink and black using intarsia. There is no graph to follow, as all the stripes are simply worked in even columns after the cast-on row.

Begin by preparing 7 (8, 9) balls of pink and 6 (7, 8) balls of black. Cast on 59 (68, 77) stitches in the following order: 5 pink and 4 black. Repeat this 6 (7, 8) times. Finally, cast on 5 pink.

Your ribbed pattern will be only within the black columns. It is knit 1, purl 2, knit 1 on the right side in black. The rib pattern on the back of the black columns is purl 1, knit 2, purl 1. All of the pink columns will be worked in stockinette stitch, knitting on the right side and purling on the wrong side. You will interlock the yarns between the pink and black columns using intarsia as you normally would in stockinette stitch. Basically you will be repeating the instructions for row 1 and row 2 as follows:

*row 1 (right side):* With pink knit 5; with black knit 1, purl 2, knit 1. Repeat this across, ending the row by knitting 5 with pink.

*row 2 (wrong side):* With pink purl 5; with black purl 1, knit 2, purl 1. Repeat this across, ending the row by purling 5 with pink.

Be sure to interlock the pink and black yarns each time you change colors as you normally would work intarsia in stockinette stitch.

Work this pattern until the corset measures 9 (10, 11) inches—about 46 (50, 54) rows. Bind off. Begin binding off as you usually would, but remember to change to the next color of yarn 1 stitch before the end of the column. That way, when you bind off the first stitch of a new color column, you will have the correct yarn color on the needle. After binding off all stitches, take all the time needed to weave in all loose ends using a darning needle.

To create the decorative details running vertically on the pink columns, use a darning needle and the black yarn to make duplicate stitches on the center of the pink columns. Make a duplicate stitch every other row in the center of every pink column. Using the black yarn and a crochet hook, you will add a black edging to the sides of the corset to lace ribbon through for the closure. Along each of the sides of the pink columns on the edge of the corset, use the crochet hook to single crochet 23 (25, 27) times evenly along each side. On the next row, crochet holes by chaining 3 and working a single crochet into every other single crochet. Lace your ribbon by crisscrossing through these chain-3 holes. ❤

CHaPTer o4

for The arms

punk rockers have always embraced the use of military uniforms and insignia to thumb their noses at authority. we love the simplicity and boldness of the red cross symbol. wear these to your next hardcore show!

## MATERIALS

» Size 8 needles, or size required to get correct gauge
» Yarn bobbins, optional
» Row counter, optional
» Darning needle
» 1 skein black worsted-weight wool yarn (Cascade 220, 100% Peruvian Highland wool, Black, #8555)
» 1 skein off-white worsted-weight wool yarn (Cascade 220, 100% Peruvian Highland wool, Natural, #8010)
» 1 skein dark red worsted-weight wool yarn (Cascade 220, 100% Peruvian Highland wool, Ruby, #9404)

## GAUGE (IN STOCKINETTE STITCH)

» 18 stitches and 24 rows make a 4-inch square

## FINISHED MEASUREMENTS

» 4 inches by 8 inches before seaming

## SKILLS & METHODS

» Intarsia
» Stockinette stitch

feel the pain
wrist cuffs with red cross design

continued »

70

*pretty in PuNk*

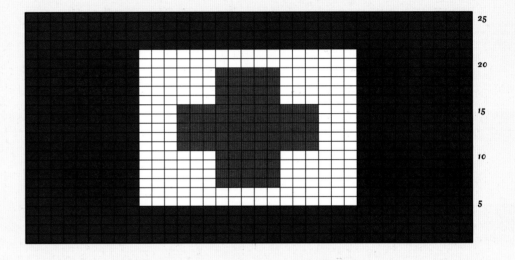

25

20

15

10

5

## FEEL THE PAIN GRAPH

This is a quick and easy project, whether you make only one or a pair! Again, the easiest way to keep your work neat when knitting intarsia is to have separate balls of yarn or separate bobbins of yarn ready at the beginning. For this one, you'll need 2 balls of black, 2 balls of white, and 1 ball of red (about 20 yards each ball). Cast on 35 stitches with black yarn. Work in stockinette stitch for 3 rows. These plus your cast-on row count as your first 4 rows as shown in the intarsia graph. On row 5, begin following the intarsia pattern by knitting 9 black stitches, attach white yarn, and knit the 17 stitches, then attach a second ball of black yarn and knit 9 stitches. Continue following the intarsia pattern, intro-ducing the red yarn on row 7 until row 21. Knit rows 22 to 25 in black yarn. Bind off in black. Use your darning needle to weave all the loose threads into the back of the knitting. Fold the wrist warmer in half lengthwise, right sides facing each other, and stitch the seam together using your darning needle. Your finished wrist warmer looks great and is so quick to knit that you can wear it right away. However, we do recommend washing it first in a little cold water and hair conditioner to improve the feel of the wool. Lay flat on a towel to dry. It's not usually necessary to block these small pieces, but if your knitting is curled up or out of shape, blocking can only help! ❤

*being punk rock doesn't mean you always have to look hard and tough. give in to your feminine side once in a while with these fuzzy pink-and-black striped warmers. reminiscent of beetlejuice, alice in wonderland, and raggedy ann, they prove that you don't have to sacrifice your quirkiness in order to be girly.*

## MATERIALS

» Size 5 needles, or size required to get correct gauge
» Row counter, optional
» Darning needle
» 1 skein pink fingering-weight mohair (Joseph Galler Yarns, Flore II, 75% kid mohair, 20% wool, 5% nylon, Light Pink, #077)
» 1 skein black fingering-weight mohair (Joseph Galler Yarns, Flore II, 75% kid mohair, 20% wool, 5% nylon, Black, #015)
» 1 skein red fingering-weight mohair (Joseph Galler Yarns, Flore II, 75% kid mohair, 20% wool, 5% nylon, Red, #064)

love
bites
striped arm warmers with heart design

## GAUGE (IN STOCKINETTE STITCH)

» 18 stitches and 28 rows make a 4-inch square

## FINISHED MEASUREMENTS

» 8 inches by 7 inches before seaming

## SKILLS & METHODS

» Fair Isle knitting
» Stockinette stitch

*continued »*

bit

## LOVE BITES GRAPH

Cast on 31 stitches in pink mohair, and work in stockinette stitch throughout, following the Love Bites graph. Work 3 rows in pink mohair. These 3 rows plus your cast-on row count as the first 4 rows of the graph. Switch to black mohair, and work 4 rows. Switch back to pink, and work 4 more rows. Switch back to black, and work 2 rows. On row 15, knit 15 stitches in black mohair. Add red mohair, and knit 1 stitch. Carry the black mohair across and above the red mohair, and knit 15 stitches in black. Follow the graph for rows 16 to 23. Work 1 row in black mohair. Work 4 rows of pink mohair alternating with 4 rows of black mohair 4 times. Finish with 2 rows of pink mohair. Bind off the third row in pink mohair. Use your darning needle to weave all of the loose threads into the back of the knitting. Fold the wrist warmer in half lengthwise, right sides facing each other, and stitch the seam together using your darning needle and a length of pink mohair. We like to start the seam at the second black row from the top. This allows more give for the wider part of the arm. Turn right-side out. ❤

55

50

45

40

35

30

25

20

15

10

5

*feel like you need a little rock and roll in your life? we've got the perfect accessories! these wrist warmers are relatively easy to knit and a riot to wear. with or without the red mohawk accent, this skull-and-crossbones pair alerts others to your dangerous side. rock on!*

## MATERIALS

» Size 5 needles
» Yarn bobbins, optional
» Row counter, optional
» Darning needle
» Size 0 crochet hook, Optional
» 1 skein black worsted-weight wool yarn (Cascade 220, 100% Peruvian Highland wool, Black, #8555)
» 1 skein white worsted-weight wool yarn (Cascade 220, 100% Peruvian Highland wool, White, #8505)
» 1 skein dark red worsted-weight wool yarn (Cascade 220, 100% Peruvian Highland wool, Ruby, #9404), optional

## GAUGE (IN STOCKINETTE STITCH)

» 24 stitches and 32 rows make a 4-inch square

# death ♥ or glory

wrist warmers with skull-and-crossbones design

## FINISHED MEASUREMENTS

» 6 inches by 7 inches before seaming

## SKILLS & METHODS

» Fringe, optional
» Intarsia
» Stockinette stitch

*continued »*

de

Let's begin with the crossbones wrist warmer. You will need 3 balls of black yarn and 2 balls of white yarn. Cast on 36 stitches in black yarn on size 5 needles. Following the intarsia graph, work 7 rows of black in stockinette stitch. These plus the cast-on row count as the first 8 rows. On row 9, knit 11 black stitches, add white and knit 2 stitches, add another black and knit 10 stitches, add another white and knit 2 stitches, and finally add another black and finish the row. Follow the intarsia design of the crossbones for rows 10 to 27. Finally, work 17 rows in black followed by 3 rows in white. Bind off in white. Use your darning needle to weave all of the loose threads into the back into the knitting. Fold the wrist warmer in half lengthwise, right sides facing each other, and stitch the seam together using your darning needle and a length of black yarn. We like to start the seam right below the white top trim. This allows more give for the wider part of the arm. Turn right-side out, and voilà!

Similarly, for the skull wrist warmer, cast on 36 stitches in black yarn on size 5 needles. Following the intarsia graph, work 7 rows in stockinette stitch. The intarsia design for the skull begins on the ninth row as well. Follow the intarsia design of the skull to the end. Then work 16 rows in black followed by 3 rows in white. Bind off in white. Weave in the loose ends, stitch the seam together, and turn right-side out. Again, start the seam right below the white top trim.

For the optional Mohawk, cut ten 3-inch strands of red yarn. Use a size 0 crochet hook to create a fringe of individual red strands above the forehead of the skull. Space the red strands evenly around the crown of the skull, approximately 1 stitch above the skull. Make sure each fringe knot faces the top edge of the skull so that the yarn lies correctly. This is the same method used for attaching fringe to the edge of a scarf. See glossary for details. To achieve the fuzzy texture, agitate and massage both wrist warmers in alternating baths of cold water and hot water, with conditioner, 3 times. Lay flat on a towel to dry. Fluff Mohawk. ♥

## SKULL GRAPH

## CROSSBONES GRAPH

45
40
35
30
25
20
15
10
5

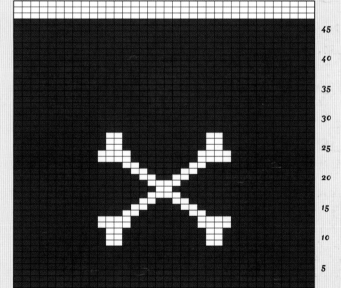

45
40
35
30
25
20
15
10
5

death
or glory

as teenagers, we often shopped at army surplus stores looking for inexpensive yet subversive fashion finds. twenty years later, camouflage can be seen everywhere from runway shows to street wear. it is a great design for mixing punk-rock attitude with high fashion sensibility.

# combat rocker

### felted camouflage lace-up arm warmers

## MATERIALS

» Size 5 needles
» Yarn bobbins, optional
» Row counter, optional
» Darning needle
» 1 skein dark olive green worsted-weight wool yarn (Cascade 220, 100% Peruvian Highland wool, Yakima Heather, #9459)
» 1 skein pale olive green worsted-weight wool yarn (Cascade 220, 100% Peruvian Highland wool, Irelande, #2429)
» 1 skein black worsted-weight wool yarn (Cascade 220, 100% Peruvian Highland wool, Black, #8555)
» 1 skein tan worsted-weight wool yarn (Cascade 220, 100% Peruvian Highland wool, Camel, #8622)
» 6 yards thin black velvet ribbon or cord

## GAUGE (IN STOCKINETTE STITCH)

» 24 stitches and 32 rows make a 4-inch square (before felting)

## FINISHED MEASUREMENTS

» 9 inches by $7^1/_2$ inches at the widest and $5^1/_2$ inches at the narrowest after felting

## SKILLS & METHODS

» Felting
» Intarsia
» Stockinette stitch

continued »

80

*pretty in PuNk*

There is a lot of color-switching in this pattern, so we suggest you begin by preparing 4 balls of dark olive green yarn, 4 balls of pale olive green yarn, 3 balls of black yarn, and 5 balls of tan yarn before you actually start knitting. Cast on 50 stitches in pale olive green yarn. Note: The cast-on row is the first row shown in the camouflage intarsia graph. Work in stockinette stitch throughout. There are 7 sets of decreases in this project, which you can make simply by knitting 2 stitches together. We suggest knitting the second and third stitches together as well as the second- and third-to-last stitches in rows 13, 24, 35, 46, 57, 68, and 79. This will retain a clean edge. Follow the intarsia graph to the end. Bind off row 90 in pale olive green. Weave all the loose threads into the back of the knitting. This takes a bit of time but is necessary so your stitches do not come apart in the wash. To felt, throw the arm warmers into a washing machine, and run through 2 hot cycles, without detergent or conditioner. As soon as you take them out, pin them to a pillow or a blocking board so that they dry flat and straight. To finish, thread ribbon or cord of your choice through with a darning needle and lace up. Trim ribbon or cord as needed.

**hint:** If this seems too challenging, we have found that there are many variegated, multicolor yarns available, even olive green–toned instant camouflage. Feel free to skip the intarsia entirely, and just follow the sets of stitches, rows, and decreases for instant gratification! ❤

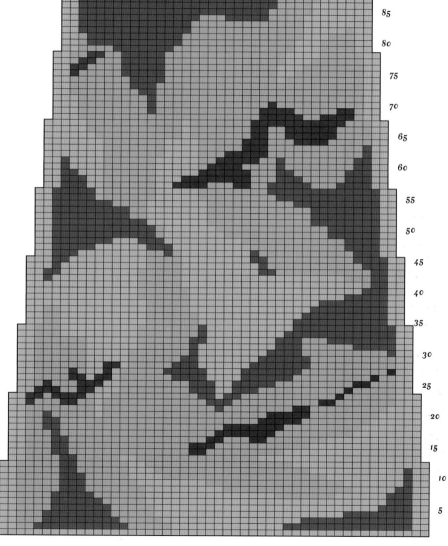

**CAMOUFLAGE GRAPH**

CHaPTer o5

FoR THE bum

nineteen-seventies punk rockers customized their denim and leather jackets by cutting off the sleeves and adding patches of their favorite bands and slogans. reminiscent of those "kutten," our bum patch adds flair to your favorite jeans or pants. we chose the historic american roadway, but we hope that this project inspires you to design your own custom bum patches!

## MATERIALS

» Size 5 needles, or size required to get correct gauge
» Row counter, optional
» Size 0 crochet hook
» Darning needle
» 1 skein white worsted-weight wool yarn (Cascade 220, 100% Peruvian Highland wool, White, #8505)
» 1 skein black worsted-weight wool yarn (Cascade 220, 100% Peruvian Highland wool, Black, #8555)

## GAUGE [IN STOCKINETTE STITCH]

» 24 stitches and 32 rows make a 4-inch square

## FINISHED MEASUREMENTS

» Approximately 6 inches by 6 inches

bum patch

pocket patch featuring route 66 design

## SKILLS & METHODS

» Crochet (single)
» Fair Isle knitting
» Stockinette stitch

*continued »*

We measured the back pockets of several pairs of jeans to come up with the shape and measurements for this patch. It should fit most. Work this piece in stockinette stitch, following the Route 66 graph, as we did, because decreases tend to look neater than increases. After you have knit the piece, we suggest finishing it off with a single crochet trim all around the perimeter for a defining edge.

Cast on 35 stitches in white yarn. Begin following the Route 66 graph. On row 2, purl 17 stitches in white, add black and purl 1 stitch, carry the white yarn across the back of the knitting, and purl 17 stitches. Continue following the graph. Note: There will be 3 sets of decreases between rows 3 and 40. Purl together the second and third stitches as well the second- and third-to-last stitches on rows 10, 20, and 30; 29 stitches remain. Follow the graph to the end of row 40.

To create the triangular point of the patch, work rows 41 through 48 in stockinette stitch while binding off the first 5 stitches of rows 41, 42, and 43. On the next row, bind off the first 6 stitches. You should have 8 stitches remaining. Knit 2 together 4 times across the next row until 4 stitches remain. Purl the next row. Finally, knit 2 together twice and bind off.

For a defining border, single crochet black yarn into every other stitch around the perimeter of the piece. Crochet 3 times into each of the 4 corners and the bottom point to create sharp corners. Repeat if you would like to create another patch for the second back pocket of your jeans or pants.

To finish, use your darning needle to weave all loose ends into the back of the knitting. Agitate the piece in alternating baths of cold water and hot water, with conditioner, 3 times. Wring out excess water, and roll in a towel. Pin flat to dry overnight. Press with a hot iron. Finally, sew the patch(es) onto the back pocket(s) of your favorite pair of jeans or pants. Don't worry if the patch doesn't fit the pocket exactly. Simply line up the edges of the pocket with the edges of the patch and sew. Throw the jeans into the washing machine for one hot wash cycle, and the patch will felt, shrinking slightly to fit. ❤

# ROUTE 66 GRAPH

all hail british fashion designer vivienne westwood. her ingenious designs, created for the sex pistols and the new york dolls, inspired our knit version of the bum flap, which she used often in her bondage suits. the bold monochromatic union-jack design pays homage to the origin of the style. decorate as you like, with hardware, safety pins, or grommets.

## MATERIALS

» Size 10 1/2 needles, or size required to get correct gauge
» Yarn bobbins, optional
» Row counter, optional
» 3 hook fasteners or safety pins
» 1 skein black bulky-weight wool yarn (Brown Sheep Co., Lamb's Pride Bulky, 85% wool, 15% mohair, Onyx, M05)
» 1 skein charcoal bulky-weight wool yarn (Brown Sheep Co., Lamb's Pride Bulky, 85% wool, 15% mohair, Charcoal Heather, M04)
» 1 skein light gray bulky-weight wool yarn (Brown Sheep Co., Lamb's Pride Bulky, 85% wool, 15% mohair, Silver Sliver, M130)

## GAUGE (IN STOCKINETTE STITCH)

» 12 stitches and 20 rows make a 4-inch square

# union jack

a-line bum flap with british flag design and metal fasteners

## FINISHED MEASUREMENTS

» 11 inches across top, 16 1/4 inches across bottom, and 9 1/2 inches vertically

## SKILLS & METHODS

» Intarsia
» Stockinette stitch

continued »

union
jack *continued*

**90**

...........

*pretty* in *PuNk*

## UNION JACK GRAPH

This pattern is knit from the bottom of the flap up, mainly because decreasing stitches is easier and looks neater. Cast on 54 stitches in black yarn. Knit 1 row in black. This plus your cast on row counts as the first 2 rows as shown on the Union Jack intarsia graph. Continue the design in stockinette, introducing the various balls of yarn corresponding to the colors on the graph. Your 6 sets of decreases will be on rows 10, 17, 24, 31, 38, and 45. In other words, knit 2 together at the beginning and end of these decrease rows. We prefer to knit together the second and third stitches and the second- and third-to-last stitches in each decrease row. This creates a cleaner finish than knitting together the first and last 2 stitches. You will have 42 stitches remaining in row 48 if you decreased properly. Bind off in black.

Depending on how tightly you knit, your finished project may now look all curled up. This is perfectly normal. Simply wash the bum flap in cold water with conditioner. Lightly wring out the excess water, lay flat on a towel, and roll up in the towel to wring out as much water as possible. At this point you can block the item. We like to use a pillow covered with a towel, but of course you can use a blocking board. Simply place the damp item flat on the pillow, and use quilting pins or safety pins to hold it in place until it's absolutely dry.

Once dried, attach 3 hook fasteners or safety pins to the top of your flap and then attach to the back of your jeans belt loops. We used metal hook and key rings with chains for ours. ❤

*anglomania continues with this rectangular bum flap. a hallmark of punk style was to take and use conventional items and symbolism out of context. here we used a traditional navy blue military uniform color and combined it with a classic gold queen's crown. the result is not only stylish but will also keep you warm on those long nights when you're sitting out for concert tickets.*

### MATERIALS

» Size 7 needles, or size required to get correct gauge
» Row counter, optional
» Darning needle
» 3 metal key holders
» 1 skein navy blue worsted-weight wool yarn (Cascade 220, 100% Peruvian Highland wool, Navy, #8393)
» 2 skeins gold plied worsted-weight metallic yarn (Filatura Di Crosa's New Smoking, 65% viscose, 35% polyester, #1)

### GAUGE (IN STOCKINETTE STITCH)

» 20 stitches and 24 rows make a 4-inch square before wetting and blocking

### FINISHED MEASUREMENTS

» 16 inches by 9 inches before wetting and blocking

### SKILLS & METHODS

» Crochet (single)
» Fair Isle knitting
» Stockinette stitch

## dethroned

rectangular bum flap with queen's crown design and metal fasteners

*continued »*

*pretty in PuNk*

35
30
25
20
15
10

**CROWN GRAPH**

This item is worked with 1 strand of the navy blue yarn and 2 strands of the metallic gold yarn. Cast on 79 stitches in navy blue yarn. Work 10 rows in stockinette stitch. Please note that the crown graph only shows the 31 center stitches of rows 10 through 35. The 24 stitches on either side of the graph are knit or purled in navy blue yarn. On row 11, begin following the graph by knitting 34 stitches in navy blue yarn, add 2 strands of metallic gold yarn and knit 11 stitches, and then carry the navy blue yarn across the back of the knitting and knit 34 stitches. Follow the graph to the end of row 35, remembering to either knit or purl 24 stitches in navy blue yarn on either side of the graph. Please note that the

crosses on either side of the crown at rows 19 through 21 were worked with separate pieces of yarn to prevent puckering in the finished fabric. Work rows 35 to 55 with the navy blue yarn in stockinette stitch. Bind off. Weave the loose ends into the back of the knitting. To even out the stitches, agitate the piece in an alternating bath of hot and cold water, with conditioner, 3 times. Wring out and roll up in a towel to remove excess water. Pin flat to a pillow or blocking board, and let dry overnight. Remove the next day, and sew 1 metal key holder to the top right corner, 1 to the center, and 1 to the top left corner. A great resource for key holders is Toho Shoji N.Y. Be sure to look it up on our Materials page! ♥

*a micro-mini with a twist! we feature a traditional preppy argyle on the front of this feminine creation. so versatile, you can wear it as a tube top too! don't worry: you can still wear combat boots or creepers with your ensemble.*

## MATERIALS

» 24-inch size 7 circular needle, or size required to get correct gauge
» Size 7 straight needles
» Row counter, optional
» Stitch holders
» Darning needle
» 2 (3, 3) skeins red worsted-weight yarn (Rowan Cashsoft Aran, 57% extrafine merino, 33% microfiber, 10% cashmere, Poppy, #512)
» 1 skein gray worsted-weight yarn (Rowan Cashsoft Aran, 57% extrafine merino, 33% microfiber, 10% cashmere, Thunder, #518)
» 1 skein black worsted-weight yarn (Rowan Cashsoft Aran, 57% extrafine merino, 33% microfiber, 10% cashmere, Black, #519)
» 1 yard white worsted-weight yarn (Rowan Cashsoft Aran, 57% extrafine merino, 33% microfiber, 10% cashmere, Cream, #500)
» 1 yard of ¹/₂-inch-wide elastic for band

## GAUGE (IN STOCKINETTE STITCH)

» 17 stitches and 23 rows make a 4-inch square

## FINISHED MEASUREMENTS (SIZES MEDIUM AND LARGE ARE GIVEN IN PARENTHESES)

» 25 (29, 33 ¹/₂) inches in circumference by 11 (12, 13) inches long

## SKILLS & METHODS

» Intarsia
» Stockinette stitch

ready
steady go
miniskirt with argyle design and flounce

*continued »*

This skirt is knit mostly in the round on circular needles, except for the intarsia panel shown on the diamond graph. You will knit from the waist down, paying close attention to the first several rounds, which are important for creating the waistband. Begin by casting on 106 (124, 142) stitches of red on the circular needle using the double cast-on method. Note that using other cast-on methods may result in a narrow casing for the waistband. Place a marker, and join the beginning and end of the round, making sure that the cast-on stitches are not twisted. Knit 3 rounds, then purl 1 round. The ridge created by the purl round on the right side will allow you to fold the waistband over so that you can sew in the elastic band later.

Continue knitting the skirt in the round for another 12 (15, 18) rounds, and then prepare to work the argyle panel in flat knitting by transferring the first 43 stitches onto a straight needle and dividing the gray yarn into 2 separate balls. Work the intarsia graph panel in the front center of the skirt on these 43 stitches. Keep the remaining 63 (81, 99) stitches on the circular needles, or if you are not comfortable working that way, transfer them onto a large stitch holder. When you are finished with the argyles as graphed, place the argyle panel on stitch holders. Work the other 63 (81, 99) stitches flat in stockinette stitch until this section measures the same length as the front panel, then place all of the stitches on the circular needle and begin working in the round again. Knit every round (stockinette stitch) for another 12 (15, 18) rows, until the piece measures 9 (10, 11) inches from the purled ridge.

At this point, you will create the flounce of the skirt. This is done by working in the round in the following manner. Knit 1, yarn over all around, 212 (248, 284) stitches. On the next round, purl as follows: purl into each stitch, and purl twice into each yarn over, by purling into the front and back of the loop. At the end of this round you will have 318 (372, 426) stitches. Knit the next 12 rounds (stockinette stitch), and bind off.

With a darning needle and red yarn, use mattress stitch to seam up the 2 slits at either side of the argyle pattern. Then, using the white yarn and the darning needle, stitch 2 diamond outlines between the 3 intarsia argyles. Finally, cut the elastic to 26 (30, 32 $^1/_2$) inches or to 1 inch more than the desired length, and join the ends with a 1-inch overlap, being careful not to twist. Place it on the wrong side of the skirt fabric, and fold the waistband over it to the inside, so that the purl round is now the top edge of the skirt. Sew the waistband down with red yarn all around the elastic band, and your skirt is finished! If the flounce of the skirt curls up, wet the knitted fabric, gently wring it out, and lay it flat on a towel to dry. ❤

# DIAMOND GRAPH

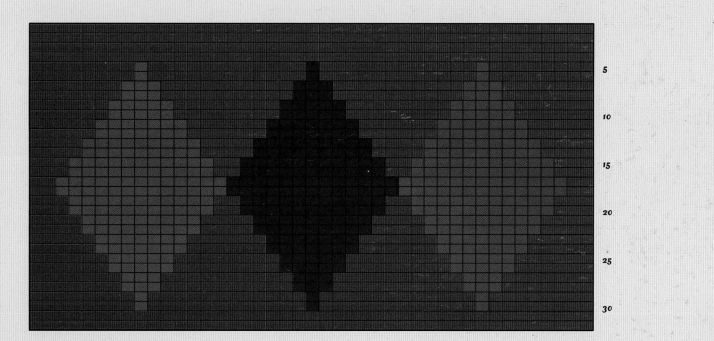

5
10
15
20
25
30

ready
steady go

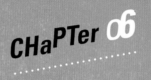

CHaPTer o6

FoR the
rest

FoR the

we confess we were never huge fans of the who, but we watched quadrophenia because sting was in it! we also love the mod scene and bold bull's-eye design and so incorporated it into this small tote bag.

## MATERIALS

» Size 7 needles, or size required to get correct gauge
» Double-pointed needles one size larger
» Yarn bobbins, optional
» Crochet hook or darning needle
» 1 skein white worsted-weight yarn (Cascade, 100% Peruvian Highland wool, White, #8505)
» 1 skein blue worsted-weight yarn (Cascade, 100% Peruvian Highland wool, Blue Velvet, #7818)
» 1 skein red worsted-weight yarn (Cascade, 100% Peruvian Highland wool, Christmas Red, #8895)

## GAUGE [IN STOCKINETTE STITCH]

» 20 stitches and 25 rows make a 4-inch square on smaller needles before felting

## FINISHED MEASUREMENTS

» 9 inches by 12 inches before felting; 9 inches by 9 inches after felting

mini
mod
small felted tote bag with mod target design

## SKILLS & METHODS

» Felting
» I-cord
» Intarsia
» Stockinette stitch

*continued »*

*pretty in PuNk*

## TARGET GRAPH

To begin this one, separate your yarn into 4 balls or bobbins of the white yarn, 2 balls or bobbins of the blue, and just 1 red. Cast on 46 stitches with the regular needles and white yarn using the double cast-on method. Count this as your first row, and begin following the target intarsia graph, working in stockinette stitch throughout. Your last row of white should be your bind-off row. This is the front of the bag.

For the back piece, you can repeat as for the front, or if you prefer, simply cast on 46 stitches in white and knit in all white for 75 rows in stockinette stitch, then bind off. This depends on whether you'd like the graphic on both sides of the bag. Put the 2 pieces together with the right sides facing, and sew along the sides and bottom of the bag, using either a crochet hook or darning needle, whichever method you prefer. Your bag is now sewn inside out. Just turn it right-side out in order to attach the tote handles. With the right side facing you, pick up 5 stitches beginning at the eighth stitch from the left with the white yarn and double-pointed needles. Work stockinette stitch for 3 rows, then

knit the I-cord (see the glossary for details) for about 24 inches. Then work 3 more regular stockinette stitch rows, and sew onto the right side. You should attach the I-cord so that it is symmetrical to the left side, with the right side of the handle at the eighth stitch from the right side of the bag. Repeat the same thing for the handle on the other side of the bag. Using a crochet hook or yarn needle, weave in all loose ends. Throw the finished bag into a washing machine along with a pair of old jeans for agitation, and wash on a hot wash setting with a cold rinse, without detergent or conditioner. Your finished bag will shrink to about 9 inches wide by 9 inches high, and the finished fabric will be smooth and sturdy! ❤

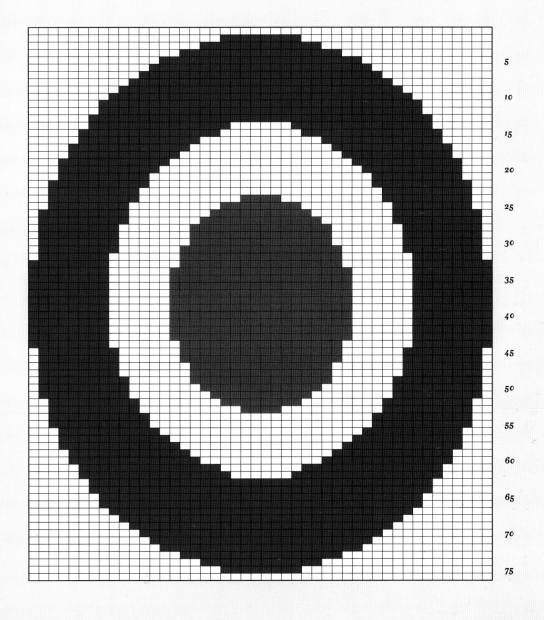

mini

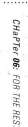

*this large courier-style bag can be worn diagonally on the shoulder and is inspired by old army surplus bags. our version is updated to include contrast colors and a punk-rock silhouette with a raised mohawk accent, which complements our hats.*

## MATERIALS

» Size 11 needles, or size required to get correct gauge
» Yarn bobbins, optional
» Row counter, optional
» Size 1 crochet hook
» Darning needle
» 1 skein olive green bulky-weight wool yarn (Brown Sheep Co., Lamb's Pride Bulky, 85% wool, 15% mohair, Oregano, M113)
» 1 skein beige bulky-weight wool yarn (Brown Sheep Co., Lamb's Pride Bulky, 85% wool, 15% mohair, Oatmeal, M115)
» 1 skein off-white bulky-weight wool yarn (Brown Sheep Co., Lamb's Pride Bulky, 85% wool, 15% mohair, Creme, M10)

## GAUGE (IN STOCKINETTE STITCH)

» 12 stitches and 16 rows make a 4-inch square, before felting

## FINISHED MEASUREMENTS

» Bag 11 inches by $1^{1}/_{2}$ inches by 13 inches, strap $41^{1}/_{2}$ inches by 2 inches, both after felting

## SKILLS & METHODS

» Crochet (single)
» Felting
» Fringe
» Intarsia
» Stockinette stitch

# anarchist

large felted courier bag with punk mohawk silhouette

*continued »*

This bag is made up of 3 simple pieces, 1 rectangle with the intarsia design for the front, 1 plain olive green rectangle for the back, and 1 very long beige rectangle for the shoulder strap and seam. It is assembled and finished with a single crochet using the olive green yarn.

In preparation for the front panel, divide the olive green yarn into 2 balls. Cast on 40 stitches on regular needles in the following order: 2 in olive green, 36 beige, and 2 olive green again. Work in stockinette stitch throughout, slipping the first stitch in each row. This will be important when seaming together the bag. The cast-on row is the first row of the silhouette intarsia graph. Work 62 more rows, following the intarsia graph. Then work 7 rows in olive green. Bind off row 70 in olive green.

For the back panel, cast on 40 stitches in olive green yarn. Work 73 rows in stockinette stitch, slipping the first stitch of each row, and bind off.

For the side seam/shoulder strap, cast on 7 stitches in beige yarn. Remember again to slip the first stitch in each row. Work until the piece measures at least 82 inches. Depending on how long you like your shoulder strap, you can make it longer by adding rows or shorter by knitting fewer rows.

To assemble the bag, take the shoulder strap/seam and the front piece and join along the edge of the right side using olive green yarn and working a single crochet in each row. Continue to single crochet across the bottom, along the other side, and around the edge of the shoulder strap, even where it does not connect to the bag in order to create the thin stripe of olive green trim on the shoulder strap. Do the same with the back panel. This is an intentional raised seam. Turn the bag inside out, and seam together the head and tail of the shoulder strap/seam with beige yarn. This seam should be invisible.

To add the raised Mohawk accent to the silhouette on the front of the bag, you will be cutting individual strands to form fringes. First, cut approximately eighty 6-inch-long strands of beige yarn. Each fringe set consists of 4 strands of yarn, and you will need approximately 16 to 19 sets for the back row of the Mohawk detail. Lay the bag flat on your lap with the top of the silhouette facing you. To make a fringe, insert your crochet hook, pull through, and knot the set. (See the glossary for details). The fringe knot should face away from you. Attach the remaining fringe sets desired every 2 or 3 stitches along the crown of the head silhouette. (Our starting point for the back row was the ninth stitch in row 54.) For the front row of the Mohawk, cut approximately 26 strands of beige yarn and 13 strands of off-white yarn. You should make approximately 11 to 13 sets of fringe consisting of 2 strands of beige and 1 in off-white. Attach these sets as for the back row, to your liking. (Start at the eighth stitch in row 52.) Feel free to trim the Mohawk "hair" to your liking.

To felt, throw the finished bag into a washing machine for 1 wash on a warm cycle, without detergent or conditioner. When you take it out, separate each Mohawk strand by grabbing 1 strand in each hand and pulling them apart, down to the knot. This will create a fluffy and full finished look. You may also need to block the shoulder strap of the bag if you find that it is curling. ❤

SILHOUETTE GRAPH

*CHaPTer 06: FOR THE REST*

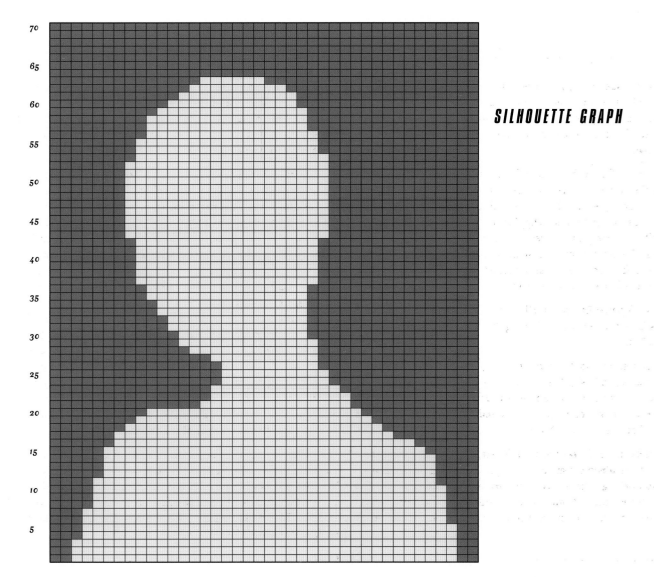

what anglophile's collection would be complete without a hound's-tooth-patterned accessory? this rectangular clutch bag features a bold red-and-black enlarged hound's-tooth. it can be used as a make-up bag or to stow necessary items for a night on the town.

## MATERIALS

» Size 10 1/2 straight needles, or size required to get correct gauge
» Double-pointed needles one size larger
» Darning needle
» 12-inch-long black zipper
» 1 skein red bulky-weight wool yarn (Brown Sheep Co., Lamb's Pride Bulky, 85% wool, 15% mohair, Ruby Red, M180)
» 1 skein black bulky-weight wool yarn (Brown Sheep Co., Lamb's Pride Bulky, 85% wool, 15% mohair, Onyx, M05)

## GAUGE (IN ONE-COLOR STOCKINETTE STITCH)

» 13 stitches and 17 rows make a 4-inch square on smaller needles

## FINISHED MEASUREMENTS

» 10 inches by 7 1/2 inches after seaming

## SKILLS & METHODS

» Fair Isle knitting
» I-cord
» Stockinette stitch

# rockabilly riot ♥

clutch bag with hound's-tooth pattern

*continued »*

*pretty* in PuNk

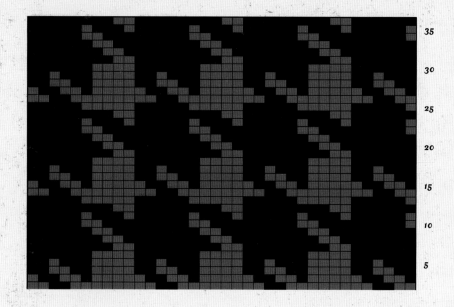

## HOUND'S-TOOTH GRAPH

35

30

25

20

15

10

5

This bag knits up very quickly and is made of 2 rectangles. The back of the bag is all red and worked in stockinette stitch. Simply cast on 36 stitches in red, and work for 35 rows. Bind off. The front of the bag is knit in stockinette stitch as well. Simply pick up stitches from along the cast-on edge of the back of the bag using the red yarn. You will need 1 ball of red and 1 ball of black to work the hound's-tooth graph using the Fair Isle technique to carry the colors across on the wrong side. Follow the graph, and

bind off using the red yarn. With a darning needle and red yarn, seam the 2 sides of the bag together using mattress stitch.

For the final touches, cast on 3 stitches, and use the double-pointed needles to create a 12-inch-long I-cord. Attach this I-cord to make a loop at 1 end of the top opening. Finally, sew a black 12-inch-long zipper across the top of the bag. Your clutch bag is ready! ❤

y

*resources*

### BIND OFF

When finishing your project or a portion of your project, this is how you get the live stitches off your needle and prevent the work from unraveling. When binding off during a knit row (right side of the fabric facing you), hold the knitting in your left hand, and use your right needle to knit two stitches. Now pass the first stitch on your right-hand needle over the second stitch and off the needle. Continue this pattern of knitting a stitch from the left-hand needle and passing the first stitch over the second stitch on the right-hand needle until only one stitch remains on your right-hand needle. Then cut the yarn, leaving about a 6-inch tail, and pull the yarn through.

### BLOCKING

Blocking is a way of setting finished knitted items or pieces after they are completed. In this book, we primarily wet the fabric either by washing or rinsing with a conditioner bath, then gently remove the water by rolling in a towel before blocking. The knitted item is then placed on a blocking board (we also use a pillow covered by a towel) and pinned in place so that it dries without the curling, uneven texture that sometimes appears in hand knitting.

### CASTING ON

There are various ways to cast on the foundation row of knitting. In the single-yarn method (also called the knitted cast-on), a slipknot is made in the yarn, about 6 inches from its end. The slipknot is placed on the left-hand needle, and then using the right-hand needle you begin to knit the slipknot. Just before the knot would be slipped off the left-hand needle during knitting, the loop created is transferred back onto the left-hand needle instead. This is repeated until the desired number of stitches appears on the left-hand needle.

In the double cast-on method (also called the continental or long-tail cast-on), the slipknot is placed a yard or a few yards from the end of the yarn (depending on the number of desired stitches), and only one needle is used. A good rule of thumb is to pull about three times the width of the piece plus a little more. The slipknot is placed on the needle, which is held in one hand while the two dangling strands of yarn are held in the other hand with the cut end of the yarn looped over your thumb and the yarn attached to the ball looped over your index finger. Stitches are cast on by taking the needle up through the thumb loop, over the index finger loop, and down through it, then pulling the new loop back through the thumb loop. Drop the loop off your thumb, and pull the two strands taut. At this point a stitch has been cast on. This is repeated to get the desired number of stitches.

### CROCHET

Crocheting is a method of creating fabric using yarn and a single hook. A foundation of chains (or existing knitting) is used as a base. The hook is simply inserted into a chain or knitted stitch, then a loop is wrapped around the hook and pulled through one loop to begin a single crochet. Finally, a loop is wrapped and pulled through the two loops to complete the single crochet, and in that way a stitch has been crocheted. A stitch can be single crocheted (one loop of yarn is wrapped), double crocheted (two loops of yarn are wrapped), or triple crocheted (three loops are wrapped). A combination of these stitches and many others is used in crochet to create lacework. In this book, it is primarily used to join seams and for some very basic edging.

## DECREASE

A decrease is a way of reducing stitches on a row by knitting two together or purling two together. We recommend knitting together the second and third stitches in from the edges of the work instead of the first two stitches on the edge in order to maintain a smooth and clean edge.

## DROPPED STITCH

When a stitch accidentally falls off the needle, it begins to unravel the knitting, working down a vertical ladder. This can be fixed with a crochet hook, looping the steps of the ladder up and back to the knitting needle. In this book, we've dropped stitches on purpose to create a distressed look.

## DUPLICATE STITCH

To make a duplicate stitch, a darning needle and yarn are used to add contrasting color to an existing item knitted in stockinette stitch. Holding the item with the right side facing you, you will notice a pattern of V shapes created by the stockinette stitch. Focus only on the V's and not the upside down V pattern you will also see between the columns. Insert your darning needle from the wrong side in the point just below the V you intend to duplicate. Then go one above the V you intend to duplicate, pull your needle and yarn through both legs of that V above, and pull the yarn through. Finally, insert your needle down and through the original point of entry. Your needle will once again be on the wrong side of the fabric, and a duplicate stitch mimicking your knitting will have been completed.

## FAIR ISLE KNITTING

In knitting a two-color design, this is a method where only one ball of each of the colors is used on each row, no matter how many color changes the pattern calls for. Whenever the design requires a different color within a row, the yarn is carried across the back of the knitting. This method is generally recommended only for two-color designs and designs where the yarn changes occur within a few stitches of each other. For larger designs where there are more than five to ten stitches to carry yarn across, it not recommended to use Fair Isle, as you will have difficulty maintaining proper tension across the back of the fabric.

## FELTING

Agitating wool so that it becomes matted is the art of felting. This is a craft that can be intricate and time-consuming, but for the projects in this book, we are simply felting finished projects by subjecting them to the washing machine, on either a hot or cold wash or a combination needed to obtain the desired effect. The finish is a firmer and sturdier fabric that is great for bags and other items. Please note that you cannot felt synthetic fibers, cotton, or superwash wool.

## FRINGE

To create a fringe, several strands of short yarn are grouped together, folded in half, and pulled through the knitted fabric with a crochet hook. The ends of the yarn are then pulled through the loop created and pulled tight, so that they remain firmly on the knitted fabric.

## GARTER STITCH

Garter stitch has a bumpy look that is created by knitting every row in flat knitting (or purling every row in flat knitting). It can be achieved when knitting in the round by placing a stitch marker at the beginning of the round and alternating knitted rounds and purled rounds. Please note that circular needles can be used in knitting without joining to form a round, and in this case you would knit every row or purl every row.

114

### I-CORD

An I-cord is a knitted tube that is created using double-pointed needles and a small number of stitches (no more than ten). A row is knit, and with the right side of the fabric facing you, the stitches are pushed back toward the right end of your needle, and the needle is moved to your left hand. The yarn is pulled across the back of the needle, and another row is knit. This is repeated until your cord grows to the desired length.

### INCREASE

There are various methods of increasing the number of stitches on a row. For the purposes of the projects in this book, we made strand increases by picking up the horizontal strand that lies between two stitches and either knitting or purling it so that it twisted, thus creating an additional stitch without making a hole.

### INTARSIA

This is a method of knitting various blocks of color with separate balls of yarn to follow a pattern of color changes or graph in stockinette stitch. When knitting and purling intarsia, you will drop your old color to the left of the stitch you just worked and bring your new color up into use to the right of the old color. This will twist the new color under the old color just once, interlocking and maintaining an even tension. It's best to practice this a few times with scrap yarn to get the hang of it.

### KNITTING IN THE ROUND

Knitting in the round is using circular needles to create a tubular finished product. After casting on the desired number of stitches and being careful not to twist any stitches in the cast-on row, you simply knit the last stitch of your cast-on to join the round. At this point, markers can be placed to signify the beginning of the round, then each round is knitted (or purled) to create a tube of stockinette stitch. In order to create a tube of garter stitch while knitting in the round, markers must be placed at the beginning of the row so that you can knit one row and then purl one row, continuing in that pattern.

### PICKING UP STITCHES

When you need to add knitting to an existing piece, you can pick up stitches along its edge instead of knitting the item separately and sewing it on. Stitches can be picked up along all edges of finished work either with a crochet hook (and transferred onto a knitting needle) or a knitting needle, which you use to pull yarn through holes in the edge of the work in a consistent manner.

### RIBBING

A combination of knitting and purling in one row, done in a pattern along vertical columns, creates ridges and makes the knitted fabric stretchy. There are infinite patterns of ribs that can be created, but some common ones are two-by-two ribs (which consist of a combination of two knits and two purls) or four-by-four ribs, and so on.

### SEAMING

There are multiple ways of joining knitted items together using a darning needle and the same yarn. When the seam will not show in the final project, you can sew two items together very simply. When a seam needs to be invisible because it will detract from the final project, you can use mattress stitch. Alternately, you can use a crochet hook to join items by crocheting them together.

### SLIP STITCH

In crochet, this is a way of joining rounds or getting to another point in the project without adding the height of the crochet stitch. You simply insert the hook through the desired stitch, pull yarn over the hook, and pull through both the stitch and the loop on your hook. In knitting, slipping a stitch is simply moving it from one needle to another without knitting or purling it.

### STOCKINETTE STITCH

Stockinette stitch is the most basic knitting pattern, creating a smooth fabric. Up close it will resemble a pattern of V's on the right side of the fabric and a bumpy set of loops on the wrong side. It is created on straight needles by alternating rows of knits and purls. It is created when knitting in the round on circular needles by knitting every row or purling every row.

### 3-NEEDLE BIND-OFF

The 3-needle bind-off is a method of binding off two pieces at the same time in order to create a smooth seam where the two pieces are joined together. It is important to have two needles with the live stitches on them, with an equal number of stitches on each needle. The two pieces should be held together with the right sides of the work facing in (inside out), then a third needle is inserted into the first stitch on each of the held needles, and the two stitches are knit together as one. This is repeated with the next stitch on the two needles. When there are two stitches on your third (right-hand needle), pass the first stitch over the second one as you would anytime you are binding off. Repeat this pattern of knitting the two next stitches of the original two needles together as one and binding off on the third needle until only one stitch remains on your right-hand needle. Then cut the yarn, leaving about a 6-inch tail, and pull the yarn through.

### WEAVING

On finished knitted items, you will have various strands of dangling yarn on the wrong side of the fabric from switching yarn, the cast-on row, and for other reasons. Using a darning needle, the dangling strands should be worked into the purl-side bumps of the fabric so that the fabric does not unravel.

### YARN OVER

These can be used to increase stitches and make decorative holes in knitting. When knitting, simply pull the yarn in front of the work between the two needle points and over the needle in your right hand before knitting the next stitch. When purling, bring yarn to the front, and loop it over the right-hand needle and back to the front again before purling the next stitch. On the next row, these can be knitted to make a hole and increase the number of stitches, or they can simply be dropped without knitting to create decorative holes without increasing the number of stitches.

## materials

### YARNS & NOTIONS

**brown sheep
yarn company**
100662 County Road 16
Mitchell, NE 69357
800.826.9136
www.brownsheep.com

**downtown yarns**
45 Avenue A
New York, NY 10009
212.995.5991
www.downtownyarns.com

**knit new york**
307 East 14th Street
New York, NY 10003
212.387.0707
www.knitnewyork.com

**patternworks**
800.438.5464
www.patternworks.com

**purl**
137 Sullivan Street
New York, NY 10012
212.420.8796
www.purlsoho.com

**school products
co., inc.**
1201 Broadway
New York, NY 10001
212.679.3516
www.schoolproducts.com

### TRIMMINGS & FINDINGS

**m&j trimming**
1008 Sixth Avenue
New York, NY 10018
212.391.6200
www.mjtrim.com

**toho shoji
(new york) inc.**
990 Sixth Avenue
New York, NY 10018
212.868.7465
www.tohoshoji-ny.com

### HELPFUL WEB SITES

www.cafepress.com
www.craftster.org
www.knitty.com
www.microrevolt.org/
    knitPro.htm
www.tie-a-tie.net

## tips

*There are several things we found stifling and frankly intimidating when we first began knitting. Through the years we've overcome these obstacles in order to fully express our creativity —especially when things we felt like doing or materials we had at hand seemed unorthodox or just plain weird. We recommend exploring your own methods, but here are a few pointers.*

### 1. YARN STORES

We've found varying levels of helpfulness at yarn stores over the years. But we've always encountered a certain amount of "know-it-all-ness" when we've asked for help. Or a doubtful look from the sales associate when we buy very large needles and very thin yarn. Nothing is as wonderful as seeing and touching the yarn yourself, but we've found the Internet to be a great alternative for buying yarn and materials, and usually at better prices! Once you've found a few brands of yarn that you enjoy working with, you can trust what you are ordering from the Internet.

### 2. YARN GAUGES/LABELS

The yarn gauges written on the label or the recommended gauges that appear next to instructions are fine if you are making something strictly by the book. However, you may want to use larger needles when creating your project because you want your finished item to have a looser stitch or you may not find the exact same yarn....Don't fret. You should always knit up a little swatch (about 10 stitches and 10 rows gives you a pretty good idea). Then simply figure out your stitches per inch and your rows per inch. You should be able to customize any instructions with a little math. Keep your swatches safety-pinned to a notebook page, along with your notes. It makes for a fun scrapbook over the years, as well as being useful!

### 3. INSTRUCTIONS/ABBREVIATIONS

The first time we encountered knitting instructions in a magazine, we wanted to cry. It looked like Greek! In order to really understand what was happening, we had to go to the explanation of abbreviations and literally rewrite the directions without any jargon or abbreviations. It seemed much easier to tackle in plain English. We hope our explanations in the book appeal to those of you who've shied away from traditional knitting in the past.

### 4. FINISHING/BLOCKING

When washing and rinsing knitted items, we prefer to use a capful of hair conditioner instead of detergent. It's mild, smells great, and improves the finish of the knitted item. This is one of those happy accidents we discovered over the years. After soaking your knitted item in a sink full of water with conditioner in it, lightly rinse and wring out the excess water, lay the item flat on a towel, and roll it up in a towel to truly wring out as much water as possible. At this point you can block the item, if necessary. Generally, you will block the item to prevent any edges from curling up. You can sometimes also correct proportional problems. For example, if an item seems too long, you can gently manipulate it width-wise through blocking. To block wet items, we like to use a pillow covered with a towel, but of course you can use a blocking board. Simply place the damp item flat on the covered pillow, and use quilting pins or safety pins to hold it in place until it's absolutely dry.

### 5. FELTING

Felting is strictly experimental territory for us. Again, it's something we discovered by taking a chance. Although there are books dedicated to the various methods of felting, this book keeps it simple. Just throw your finished item in the washing machine! Depending on what yarn was used, the outcome will be sturdier with fewer holes (and with significant shrinking). The sturdy fabric is terrific for bags. Some mild felting is also great for improving the look of intarsia, especially when there are tension inconsistencies where color switching occurs. As a general rule, we've found that repeated warm or hot water washes result in the most exaggerated results. For mild felting without overwhelming shrinking, a cold water wash or hand washing is best. Remember, you can't felt synthetic fibers or cotton. Although it's hard to predict exactly what will happen when you felt your completed item, we can assure that you'll get a similar outcome if you use the yarns we've indicated. But feel free to experiment!

# index

# acknowledgments

We would first like to thank **Martin L. Gore** of Depeche Mode for helping put Knit-Head on the map. He single-handedly introduced our handiwork to people around the world by wearing our Mohawk hat on stage throughout DM's Playing the Angel tour. We are truly honored that an artist whose work we have loved and admired for the past twenty-one years loves our work too! Thanks to the ultracool **Michele Romero** of *Entertainment Weekly* for being our biggest fan and for writing the article on us that caught Chronicle Books' attention. Thank you to the wonderful staff at Chronicle Books; our editor **Jodi Warshaw** and her assistant **Kate Prouty** for writing us that inviting e-mail and for always being so sweet and available to address endless questions from first-time authors; technical editor **Margaret Radcliffe**; copy editor **Eleanor Hampton**; managing editors **Doug Ogan** and **Evan Hulka**; production coordinator **Tera Killip**; and designer **Aya Akazawa**.

We would also like to thank our incredible photographer **Rob Benevides** for his artistic vision, tireless dedication, and stunning images. Thanks to **Eun Oh** for doing such a beautiful job on hair and makeup. Hugs and kisses to our lovely models and friends **Janicza Bravo**, **Polina Frantsena**, **Nicole Jurmo**, **Rebecca Muh**, **Eun Oh**, and **Tracy Perez**. You ladies rock! Finally, thank you to our Webmaster **Maggie Kraisamutr** for maintaining our Web site while we were busy knitting and writing; **Bryan Norton** for sharing the adorable dog Gordon; **Vincent and Mary Mallardi** for the awesome makeup at Alcone and for loaning their portable makeup mirror; **Michael and Despina Laudati** for use of their gorgeous apartment; **Baz Shailes** for loaning his tattoo gun and original flash; **Kat and Jay Flatt**, **Damian Panitz**, and **Meredith Chesney** for use of their wheels; **Natalie Pompilio** for editorial advice; and **Avi Mayorek** for Illustrator CS guidance.

### ALYCE WOULD ALSO LIKE TO ACKNOWLEDGE THE FOLLOWING PEOPLE:

My husband, **Rob**, for his limitless love, support, and encouragement. You are my soul mate, and you give me the strength to believe in myself. Thank you to my parents, **Lois and Frank Garbarini**, my brother, **Todd**, and my sister, **Beth**, for their love and support during the sometimes stressful and overwhelming process of creating this book. Thank you to **Joan and Peter Benevides** and **Jo-Ann**, **Jack**, **Victoria**, and **Jonathan Melchert** for their love and support and for understanding our absence during extraordinarily trying times. Thank you to my **colleagues at New York University**, especially **Rosanne Limoncelli**, for often complimenting me on my style and fashion sense and for supporting my artistic projects over the years. Finally, thank you to **Jaqui Milles**, my friend of twenty years and Knit-Head partner. We finally put our money where our mouths are!

### JAQUELINE WOULD ALSO LIKE TO ACKNOWLEDGE THE FOLLOWING PEOPLE:

I'd like to thank my **mom**, **dad**, **Caroline**, and **Matthew**, for putting up with me during this crazy endeavor. I don't think I would have survived the stress without you on my side, and I don't tell you often enough how much I appreciate and love you all. Many thanks to **Natalie Pompilio**, my great friend for more than twenty years and the best journalist and writer I know. Your generous help and advice on the creative writing aspect of this book was fantastic. To the boys, **Tristan** and **Liam**, for inspiring me with their boundless energy, curiosity, and imagination. To all of my terrific friends for their support and encouragement, especially **Susan Burns**, **Zubin Khan**, **Cate Blanchard**, and **Lawrence Street**. To **Mani Vassal**, and **Ali Ghalamfarsa**, thanks so much for all of your positive feedback and business suggestions. To my childhood friend **Tanya** for popping up in my life so unexpectedly this year and showing me the value of connections that can last a lifetime. A big thanks to all of my **colleagues at NYU** (my other full-time job!), especially my boss **Sheril Antonio** and my former boss **Pari Shirazi**, for their mentorship and generosity over many years. And finally to my buddy **Alyce**—my partner in crime—we've been through so much together! I'm thrilled we've enjoyed so many good times and even more thrilled that we survived some stressful times, especially this past year. We did it, woman!